CRAFT camp

Over 40 Fun Projects for Kids

LARK
New York

LARK
New York

An Imprint of Sterling Publishing
1166 Avenue of the Americas
New York, NY 10036

ISBN 978-1-4547-0900-8

Distributed in Canada by Sterling Publishing
c/o Canadian Manda Group, 664 Annette Street
Toronto, Ontario, Canada M6S 2C8
Distributed in the United Kingdom by GMC Distribution Services
Castle Place, 166 High Street, Lewes, East Sussex, England BN7 1XU
Distributed in Australia by Capricorn Link (Australia) Pty. Ltd.
P.O. Box 704, Windsor, NSW 2756, Australia

For information about custom editions, special sales, and premium
and corporate purchases, please contact Sterling Special Sales
at 800-805-5489 or specialsales@sterlingpublishing.com.

Illustrations by Sue Havens
Designed by Andrea Miller

Manufactured in China

2 4 6 8 10 9 7 5 3 1

larkcrafts.com

CONTENTS

INTRODUCTION

Welcome to camp, crafters! Here there is only one rule that must be followed: to have fun! In the following pages you will find over 40 projects that are perfect for crafters of all ages.

Whether making a multicolored piñata for a festive gathering, a tiara for a dress-up party, or a notebook to hide prized possessions, these family-fun projects are perfect for a weekend dedicated to family bonding. Most of the crafts use common household materials that are most likely lying around the house. In the Basics section, materials that may not be so common are explained.

The projects are divided into four sections that range in degree of difficulty: Badge One for projects that are geared for younger campers; Badge Two for projects that have more steps than those in Badge One; Badge Three for projects that may take a little longer to complete, in addition to receiving help from an adult; and Badge Four for crafts that are geared for older campers, as well as those in which an adult's presence is an absolute must (an Adult Supervision note is also placed on projects to alert adult supervision is required).

Whether you attempt to work through each project consecutively and earn all four badges or simply choose one that piques your interest, the one certainty is that these projects will quickly initiate the inner crafter in you and bring hours of entertainment!

BASICS

Most of the materials in the projects can be found in your home. Below are some materials that may not be as common.

Artist's canvas comes in many sizes. It is usually made of cotton and stretched over a wooden board. It is available at local craft and art-supply stores.

Butcher's twine is made from cotton and is available at supermarkets, kitchen-supply stores, and hardware stores.

Card stock, sometimes called pasteboard or cover stock," is thicker than construction paper. It comes in many colors and sizes.

Ceramic markers are used to paint, or draw, onto ceramic, porcelain, glass, and metal. They come in a variety of colors and range from fine to medium tips.

Citric acid is a weak acid that is used in canning, cheese- and candy-making, and home brewing. It can be found in supermarkets.

Craft foam is a thin and flexible sheet that comes in a variety of colors that can easily be cut with scissors or a craft knife. Sticky-backed craft foam is self-adhesive and does not require glue.

Household paraffin wax, also called baker's wax or canning wax, is used to seal jams, jellies, and preserves, as well as homemade candles. It can be found in supermarkets.

Embroidery floss, also called embroidery thread, comes in numerous colors. It consists of 6 strands, which can be separated depending on the desired stitch thickness. The most popular brands are DMC, Loops and Threads, and Prism.

Embroidery hoop is a circular hoop made from wood or plastic with screws to keep the fabric taut when embroidering.

Embroidery needle is a type of needle used for embroidery that has a long eye for holding the embroidery floss and sharp point for piercing the fabric. A larger number denote a thinner needle. The most common sizes are 3–9.

Jute rope is made from jute, a natural plant fiber, and comes in different sizes available at most craft stores.

Mod Podge is a glue, sealer, and finish—an all-in-one product. It comes in gloss, satin, or matte finishes and can be used on many surfaces, such as paper, wood, and fabric.

Plaster of Paris is a type of quick-setting plaster that becomes pliable when mixed with water and then hardens when left to dry. It is available in many craft stores.

Polymer clay is a type of modeling clay made from polymer polyvinyl chloride and comes in many colors. Once a shape is made, the clay is placed in an oven to harden.

Polymer clay glaze is a glaze that is brushed on after a clay piece has hardened, giving the piece a gloss or matte finish.

Shrink plastic comes in sheets in a variety of colors. Once a design is drawn onto the sheet with pencils, watercolors, or markers, the sheet is placed in an oven to reduce to a smaller size and harden.

Tapestry needles are used for many needlecrafts, such as cross-stitch, embroidery, crochet, and sewing. They have a blunt end and a large eye that can accommodate sewing thread, embroidery floss, and yarn. They come in a variety of sizes.

Washi tape originated in Japan and is similar to masking tape. It comes in different sizes and many colors and patterns.

LOLLIPOP YARN PAINTING

CRAFT

1

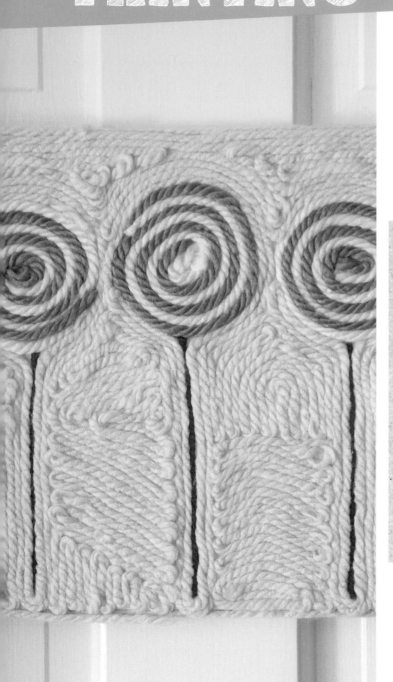

This is a great project if you have a lot of small scraps of yarn hanging around. Get inspired by lollipop colors, or use favorite colors instead.

MATERIALS AND TOOLS

9 x 12-inch (23 x 30 cm) artist's canvas

Scrap red yarn for lollipop sticks

2 skeins Lion Brand Hometown USA—
   1 each in Detroit Blue and Pittsburgh
   Yellow

1 skein Bernat Softee Chunky in
   Baby Blue

Newspaper or plastic for covering
   a work surface

Tracing paper

Pencil

Scissors

Ruler

Gel glue with a sponge-tip applicator

INSTRUCTIONS

1. Lay the canvas flat on a covered work surface with one of the 12-inch (30 cm) edges at the top. Place the ruler near the top edge and make marks at the 3-inch, 6-inch, and 9-inch (7.5, 15, and 23 cm) marks. These marks will help in placing the lollipops evenly.

2. Center at 2½-inch (6.5 cm) diameter circle over each lollipop stick. Repeat at the 6- and 9-inch (7.5 and 23 cm) marks. Don't worry if the marks aren't perfect—they can be erased and traced again!

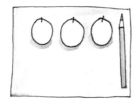

3. Lay the ruler vertically at the 3-inch (7.5 cm) mark on the canvas. Draw a straight line from the bottom of the lollipop circle to the bottom of the canvas. This will be the lollipop stick. Repeat at the 6-inch and 9-inch (15 and 23 cm) marks to give each lollipop a stick.

4. Cut three lengths of red yarn the same length as the lollipop stick lines. Spread a line of glue onto the first straight line and then place the red length of yarn on top of the glue. Repeat for the other two lollipop sticks. It's okay if the stick extends into the lollipop circle, because it can be covered with yarn swirls later.

5. Using the sponge-tip applicator, spread a small amount of glue onto the first lollipop circle. Hold the yellow and blue strands of yarn firmly next to each other without stretching them. Begin to make the lollipop swirl by laying the ends of the strands flat in the middle of the circle and wrapping the strands around the starting point.

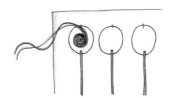

6. Continue to lay down the two strands in the circle until the entire lollipop is covered. Then cut the strands and glue the ends close to the lollipop. Repeat for the other two lollipop circles.

7. Now, get super creative! Spread glue in a specific area first. Then, using the pale blue yarn, fill in the entire background of the canvas. Start by outlining the lollipops once or twice. After that is done, work in sections as desired. Remember to spread glue in a small section of the canvas, then fill in that section with light blue yarn. See the next step for how to do this.

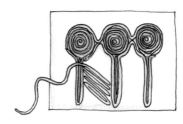

8. Cut the yarn into pieces and lay it over the glue spread on the canvas. Swirl the yarn in more circles, lay it out straight lines, or make an abstract design around the lollipops. When one section is filled, cut the yarn and start again in another section. There's no wrong way to do it! Just never cross over the lollipops or the sticks with the yarn.

9. Once the entire top of the canvas is covered, fill in the sides of the canvas so no white space shows, even when the art is hung on the wall. If a few white spots show through, just cut a piece of blue yarn and glue it into the space.

10. Let the yarn painting dry for a few hours before hanging it on the wall for everyone to see!

Cynthia Shaffer
KIDS' MASKS*

These masks are a perfect activity for a kids' party or Halloween. They can even be used as a party favor. The only restriction is your imagination!

MATERIALS AND TOOLS

- 2-mm thick craft foam in a variety of colors
- 2-mm thick sticky-backed craft foam in a variety of colors
- Templates (see pg. 121)
- Pencil
- Scissors
- Craft knife
- ⅛-inch (0.3 cm) hole punch
- Self-healing craft mat
- Coloring crayons
- Black permanent marker
- 15-inch (38 cm) elastic cord

*This project requires adult supervision.

INSTRUCTIONS

1. Trace the mask template onto the back of a sheet of craft foam and cut out with scissors. With the help of an adult, lay the mask on the self-healing mat and cut out the inside of the eyes with a craft knife. Punch holes at the side marks for the elastic cord.

2. Trace the eye templates onto a sheet of sticky-backed foam. Flip the template over to trace an opposite pair of eyes. Cut out around the eyes with the scissors and use a craft knife on a self-healing mat to cut out the inside of the eyes (again with an adult's help).

3. Peel the paper off the back of each eye and stick it onto the mask.

4. Use a coloring crayon to add details to the mask. For a girl, color in eye shadow above the eyes. Outline the eyes and draw eyelashes with a black permanent marker. For a boy, outline the eyes and draw eyelashes.

5. Repeat steps 2 and 3 for the eyebrows, glasses, hair, and crown.

6. Poke the elastic cord into the holes at the side of the mask from the outside in. Knot the elastic cord on the inside of the mask at each side. Try on the mask before knotting the other side of the cord to be sure it will be neither too tight nor too loose.

TIP

Cut out a mask and change the parts and pieces as desired. The sticky foam can be removed and the pieces can be interchanged and used over again.

Jennifer Rodriguez

ROBOT BOOKMARK*

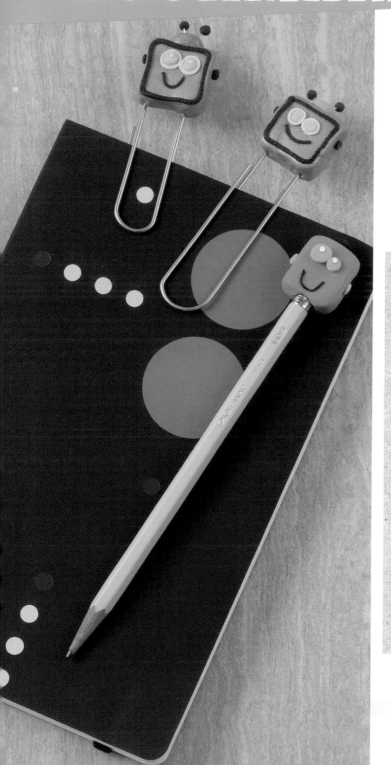

The possibilities with polymer clay are endless. Transform those extra paper clips lying around into fun, creative, and endless variations of school supplies and decorations.

MATERIALS AND TOOLS

Jumbo paper clip bookmark blank; about 3½ inches (9 cm) long
½-inch (1.3-cm) cube of sparkly silver polymer clay
¼-inch (0.6-cm) cube of black polymer clay
⅛-inch (0.3-cm) cube of light blue polymer clay
Scrap of white polymer clay
Wire cutter
Toothpick
2 small wires, 2–3 inches (5–7.5 cm)
Baby wipes
Small ceramic tile
Toaster oven
Oven mitts
Clear polymer clay glaze
Small craft paintbrush

*This project requires adult supervision.

INSTRUCTIONS

1. Ask an adult to preheat the toaster oven to 230ºF (110ºC). Condition the silver clay by rolling and pinching it until it becomes warm and soft. Pinch off a very small amount of silver clay to be used in step 2. Shape the large piece of silver clay into a cube (the robot's head) with the bookmark base sandwiched inside. Clean your hands.

TIP

Use baby wipes to clean your hands very well after using each color clay. This will prevent color transfer from one clay to another.

2. Roll the remaining small silver clay into a ball, slightly flatten one end to make it look like a small dome, and gently press it to the top of the robot head.

3. Cut the wire into two ¼ inch (0.6 cm) pieces. Insert the two small wires on an angle into each side of the dome.

4. Condition the black clay until it is soft and warm. Divide the clay in half. Divide one half into four small pieces and roll into them into balls. Place a ball of black clay on the end of each wire on the head. Place a ball of black clay on either side of the robot head to look like ear bolts.

5. Divide other half of the black clay into two pieces. Roll the first piece of clay into a very thin snake. Place the snake just inside all 4 edges of the robot head. Roll the last bit of black clay into a very thin, small snake. Shape it into a smile and carefully press onto the robot face. Clean your hands.

6. Condition the blue clay until it is soft and warm. Cut the clay into two pieces and roll them into balls. Slightly flatten them and gently press onto the robot face to create eyes. Clean your hands.

7. Condition the scrap of white clay. Roll the first piece of clay into a very thing snake and wrap it around the blue clay. Cut the clay into two pieces and roll into small balls. Gently press a white ball into each blue eye.

8. Using the toothpick, add texture to the robot face by carefully making delicate indentations.

9. Place the robot bookmark on the ceramic tile and then, using oven mitts, put the tile in the oven. Bake for 15 minutes, ask an adult to remove it with oven mitts, and let it cool completely before touching it.

10. Once it has cooled completely, paint the bookmark with a small bit of polymer clay glaze to give it a shiny look and protect it.

Jennifer Rodriguez

ROBOT PENCIL TOPPER

Be the envy of your classmates with these futuristic pencil toppers.

MATERIALS AND TOOLS

Pencil
½-inch (1.3-cm) cube of orange polymer clay
⅛-inch (0.3-cm) cube of spring-green polymer clay
⅛-inch (0.3-cm) cube of black polymer clay
Scrap of white polymer clay
Dinner knife or other dull knife
Baby wipes
Small ceramic tile
Toaster oven
Oven mitts
Clear polymer clay glaze
Small craft paintbrush

INSTRUCTIONS

1. Ask an adult to preheat the toaster oven to 230ºF (110ºC). Condition the orange clay by rolling and pinching it until it becomes warm and soft. Shape the clay into a cube with the pencil eraser base sandwiched inside. This is the robot head. Clean your hands.

TIP

Use baby wipes to clean your hands very well after using each color clay. This will prevent color transfer from one clay to another.

2. Condition the black clay until it is soft and warm. Roll into a thin snake, shape it into a smile, and gently press it onto the robot face. Clean your hands.

3. Condition the green clay until it is soft and warm. Cut the clay into two pieces and roll into balls. Cut one of them into two pieces and roll into smaller balls. Slightly flatten them and gently press them onto the robot face to create eyes. Divide the remaining green clay into two pieces and roll into small balls. Place one on either side of the robot head for ear bolts.

4. Condition the scrap of white clay. Cut the clay into two pieces and roll into small balls. Gently press one into each green eye.

5. Place the pencil on the ceramic tile and then, using oven mitts, put the tile in the oven. Bake for 15 minutes, ask an adult to remove it with oven mitts, and let it cool completely before touching it.

6. Paint the cooled robot head with a small bit of polymer clay glaze to give it a shiny look and protect it.

Jennifer Rodriguez

KAWAII CLOUD PIN*

Spice up your clothing with this happy cloud.

MATERIALS AND TOOLS

½-inch (1.3-cm) cube of glittery white polymer clay
⅛-inch (0.3-cm) cube of black polymer clay
Pink chalk
Cotton swab
Baby wipes
Small ceramic tile
Toaster oven
Oven mitts
Clear polymer clay glaze
Small craft paintbrush
Super glue
1 pinback

*This project requires adult supervision.

INSTRUCTIONS

1. Ask an adult to preheat the toaster oven to 230ºF (110ºC). Condition the white clay by rolling and pinching it until it becomes warm and soft. Pinch off a very small amount of white clay to be used later in step 5. Roll both clay pieces into balls and set aside. Clean your hands.

TIP

Use baby wipes to clean your hands very well after using each color of clay. This will prevent color transfer from one clay to another.

2. Condition the black clay until it becomes soft. Pinch off a very tiny amount to be used later in step 6. Divide the remaining black clay into two pieces for eyes. Roll all three black clay pieces into balls and set aside. Clean your hands.

3. Flatten the large ball of white clay and form it into a rough cloud shape. Place the clay cloud on the ceramic tile. With your fingertip, create texture on the top.

4. Gently flatten the two larger black clay balls and carefully press them onto the clay cloud for eyes.

5. Divide the remaining small bit of white clay into two small balls and gently press one into each of the black eyes.

6. Roll the remaining small bit of black clay into a very thin, small snake and shape into a smile. Carefully press this onto the cloud.

7. Rub a bit of pink chalk on to a cotton swab and gently rub on cloud to create two rosy cheeks.

8. Using oven mitts, put the ceramic tile into the oven. Bake for 15 minutes, ask an adult to remove it with oven mitts, and let it cool completely before touching it.

9. Paint the cooled cloud with a small bit of polymer clay glaze to give it a shiny look and protect it.

10. Place a small bit of super glue on the back of cloud and press the pinback into it. Allow to dry and enjoy a cute new cloud pin!

Nora Vrba

EASY PARTY HATS

Looking for a fun party favor for your next celebration? Try these easy party hats. Use different types of masking tape to create stripes, cut the tape into little triangles, or try something fun, like googly eyes.

MATERIALS AND TOOLS

White paper coffee/ice cups (as many as desired)

Anything sticky: stickers, masking tape, googly eyes, sticky dots

Elastic cord (variety of colors and lengths)

Tassels

Pom-poms (see page 108)

Scissors or pointed knife

Small crochet hook

INSTRUCTIONS

1. Glue a tassel or pom-pom on top of the hat to make it extra festive. Your choices are endless.

2. To attach elastic cord, use scissors to pierce a hole on each side of the cup. Measure a piece of elastic cord to match the hat and person who will be wearing it. Remember to include a little more cord for the knots inside the cup. Using a crochet hook, pull the cord through on each side, making sure both ends are inside the cup. Make a knot in each end.

TIP

Sticky dots in bright colors make for very cute dotted hats.

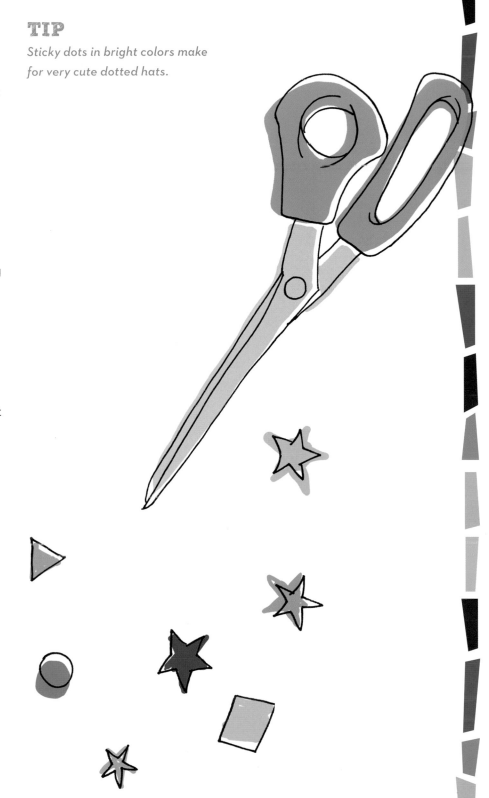

Nora Vrba

MILK-CARTON TEA LIGHT HOUSE*

Tired of throwing out empty milk cartons? Try this innovative project and let the cartons illuminate your mantle, doorstep, or table.

MATERIALS AND TOOLS

- Empty milk carton
- Matte spray paint (white was used in this project)
- Tissue paper in different colors
- Ruler
- Pencil
- Craft knife
- Scissors
- Knitting needle or long ruler
- Glue or double-sided tape
- 2 or 3 paper clips.
- Battery-operated tea light

*This project requires adult supervision.

INSTRUCTIONS

1. Carefully open the top of the carton along its seam line, rinse it well, and let dry.

2. Spray-paint the carton according to the instructions on the paint can. A few thin layers work better than one thick one.

3. Let the paint dry completely (overnight is recommended).

4. Draw windows on the house at different heights. Place them wherever desired on the front, back, or sides. Draw different kinds to create interest. Use a ruler to keep the sides straight.

5. With the help of an adult, cut the windows with a craft knife.

6. Cut the colored tracing paper slightly larger than each window opening.

7. Stick double-sided tape around the edges of the tissue paper shapes. Working from the inside of each carton, move the paper around to find the inside of each window opening and press the paper against the carton. Using a knitting needle or ruler may make this easier.

8. Close the opening with glue or double-sided tape. If you use glue, use paper clips to secure the opening while the glue dries.

9. Cut an opening at the back of the house to insert a tea light. Place the battery-operated tea light inside and wait until it is night to illuminate your milk carton tea light house!

TIP

The materials and instructions are for one house. Use various sizes of milk and dairy cartons to make a city of different-size structures. Add other materials as needed to make a city.

Mary Sinner
BIAS-TAPE TIARA

With some simple bias tape and glue, unlock your inner princess with these festive tiaras that are worthy of the most royal distinction.

MATERIALS AND TOOLS

1 fabric-covered headband
1/8-inch (0.3 cm) wide, double-fold bias tape in three colors (photo model features black, blue, and lime)
Sewing machine
White craft glue

INSTRUCTIONS

1. Cut one 13-inch (33 cm) strip from the black bias tape. Cut seven 5-inch (12.7 cm) strips from the blue bias tape. Cut fourteen 5-inch (12.7 cm) strips from the lime bias tape.

2. Fold the long black bias tape in half to find the center.

3. Center and place one blue strip on the fold.

4. Place one lime strip next to it and machine-stitch through both strips to secure them.

5. Continue placing and stitching the remaining nine strips. Cut the thread ends.

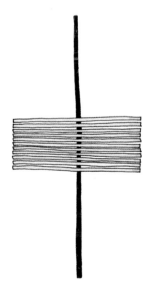

6. Turn the strip around and repeat step 4 with remaining ten strips.

7. Cut the thread ends.

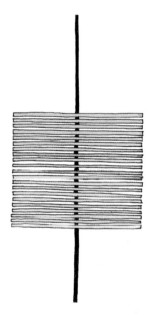

8. Apply a thin row of glue to the wrong side of the stitched strip.

9. Match the center of the strip to the center of the headband and press in place all along the strip to secure it. Let it dry completely.

10. Tie the two ends of each strip into square knots close to the headband and trim the ends.

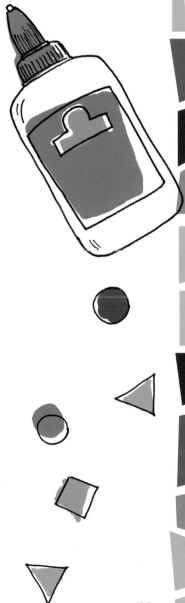

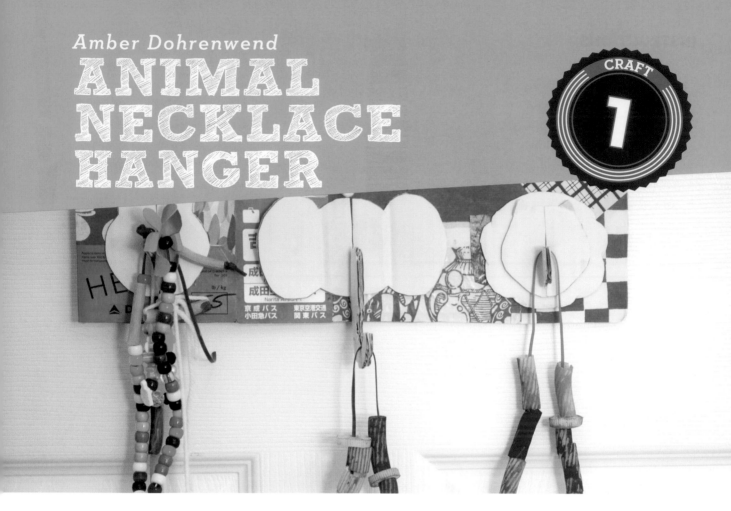

Amber Dohrenwend

ANIMAL NECKLACE HANGER

Organizing jewelry can be a beast to tame, but not with this innovative hanger. In addition to being a great space-saver idea, it also reuses old cardboard creatively.

MATERIALS AND TOOLS

- White corrugated cardboard box (a clean pizza delivery box is ideal)
- Brightly colored paper
- Old ticket stubs (for making a collage)
- White glue
- Ruler
- Pencil
- Scissors
- Paper clips
- Templates (see _pg. 122_)
- Several thumbtacks or penny nails

INSTRUCTIONS

1. Use a ruler to measure and cut a 4 x 14 inches (10.2 x 35.6 cm) rectangle for the necklace hanger backing.

2. Glue colored paper and old ticket stubs to the coat hanger backing to create a colorful collage. Allow to dry thoroughly.

3. Cut out the template pieces. Cardboard has little ridges running through it called corrugations. Trace the animal faces onto the cardboard so the corrugations are vertical, not horizontal. Trace one side of the template and then flip it over and trace the other side for all the pieces except for the lion's mane.

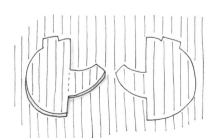

4. Follow the dotted lines on the templates to fold sections of each animal's face to create the hooks. Glue the two halves of each animal's nose together and fasten with a paper clip. Allow to dry thoroughly.

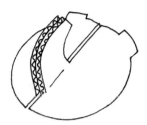

5. Space the animal heads evenly across the coat hanger backing and glue them in place.

6. Use thumbtacks or small nails to hang the animal necklace hanger in a special place.

Dora Moreland

MAGNETIC ROBOTS

CRAFT 1

Robots are cool . . . and they are even cooler when they are hanging on a refrigerator to greet you. Make them interchangeable by using different colors and patterns.

MATERIALS AND TOOLS

Several wooden rectangles
Several round craft magnets (sticky backed is recommended)
Super Glue (if not using sticky-backed craft magnets)
Pencil
Several acrylic paints in a variety of colors
Several paintbrushes, from very fine to about 1 inch (2.5 cm)
Fine-tipped marker
Mod Podge
Newspapers or plastic to cover work surface
Templates (see *pg. 123*)

INSTRUCTIONS

1. Using a pencil, draw different robot body parts (head, trunk, legs) on the different wooden rectangles. Draw freehand or cut out the templates and trace around them. Do not add details yet, just draw an outline. Use simple shapes, such as squares, circles, ovals, half-circles, or rectangles.

2. Paint the basic body parts. When the paint is dry, paint on some details—eyes, ears, neck, and mouth. Think about adding buttons to the body. Keep the shapes simple and use contrasting colors that stand out well against the base colors.

3. Draw in details, using the marker. For example, outline the robot parts to make them stand out more. Add dots for screws and squiggly or zigzag lines. Have fun!

4. Paint a layer of Mod Podge on the wooden rectangles to seal the paint. Allow to dry completely.

5. Glue craft magnets to the back of the tiles. Have fun mixing up the different parts.

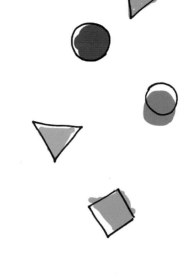

Trice Boerens

SALT-DOUGH CHOCOLATES

Whether used as a gift or a decoration, this box of chocolates is guaranteed never to get stale!

MATERIALS AND TOOLS

Salt dough (*see recipe on page 27*)
Bowl
Stirring spoon
Rolling pin
Toothpick
Dull knife
Newspaper or plastic
Medium-grit sandpaper
Light- or dark-brown, or both, pink, and white craft paint
2 paintbrushes
Water-based varnish
White craft glue
Paper candy cups
Paper box
Sewing needle
Satin cord

SALT DOUGH RECIPE

½ cup (136.5 g) salt
½ cup (120 ml) water
1 cup (120 g) flour

Stir ingredients together until the dough forms a ball. Knead the ball on a solid work surface for 5 to 10 minutes.

INSTRUCTIONS

To Construct the Chocolates

1. Roll out the dough with a rolling pin or a plastic tumbler with smooth sides until it is approximately ¾-inch (2 cm) thick.

2. Using a dull knife, cut the dough into candy shapes. Make squares ¾ inch (2 cm) and 1 inch (2.5 cm). Make circles and domes 1 inch (2.5 cm). Make rectangles and domed rectangles ¾ x 1¼ inches (2 x 3 cm). Use a toothpick to add grooves and swirls.

S Q U A R E

R E C T A N G L E

D O M E

C I R C L E

DOMED RECTANGLE

3. Place the candy forms on a paper towel and allow to dry for a day or two. The forms will shrink slightly.

4. Spread newspaper or plastic over the work surface. Sand the dried candy forms to smooth the sides and the edges.

5. Paint the candy forms and let dry.

6. Apply varnish to the candy forms and let dry.

7. Arrange the paper candy cups in the box. Apply glue to the bottom of each candy cup and press in place. Let dry.

8. Apply glue to the bottom of each candy shape and press in place. Let dry.

To Construct the Cord Handle

1. Make two marks on the short sides of the box.

2. Poke a sewing needle into each mark to make two small holes.

3. Insert one end of the satin cord into one hole and tie a knot. Trim the cord end.

4. Insert the opposite end of the cord into the remaining hole and tie a knot. Trim the cord end.

Karin Schaefer

PAPER-STRAW LETTERS

CRAFT 1

Here is a fresh way to make a "Happy Birthday" sign, a "Welcome Home" sign, or any other sign that fits a special occasion. Hang a sign (or individual letters) with a name on it outside a bedroom door. There are lots of uses for Paper-Straw Letters!

MATERIALS AND TOOLS

Heavy paper
1 box of paper straws, all one color
   or multicolored
Pencil
Scissors
Glue
Newspapers or plastic
String or masking tape (optional)

INSTRUCTIONS

1. With a pencil, draw a letter of the alphabet on heavy paper. Make the lines as thin as possible so that they will not show though the straws. To make individual letters rather than a sign, cut out each letter.

2. With scissors, cut a few straws at a time to the width of each part of the letter(s). Place the straws to the side, but laid out in the same shape as the letter(s), so they will be easy to glue in the right order.

3. Cover a work surface with newspaper or plastic. Add a thin line of glue to the straws one at a time, and place them horizontally onto the drawn or cut letter to fill in the shape. Try not to use too much glue, as it will make the background paper bend. Continue cutting the next batch of straws and gluing them until you have completed the letter(s).

4. Once the glue dries, the paper-straw letter is done.

TIP

If a big sign is needed, purchase a roll of colored paper or glue several pieces of flat paper together before adding the letters. Be sure the pieces are in a straight line. Draw out the entire name or message before attaching the straws. Add string in the corners to hang the sign, or tape it with masking tape to avoid harming painted walls.

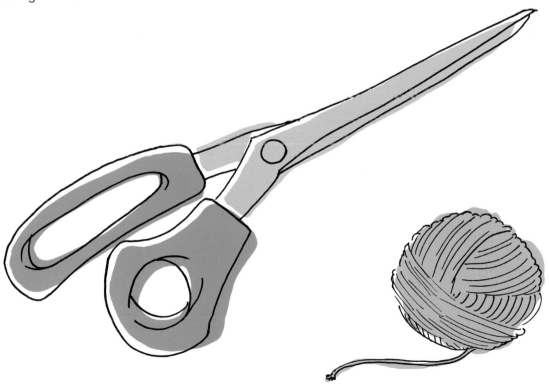

Chiara Alberetti Milott
CUPCAKE RIBBONS

CRAFT
1

Everyone is a prizewinner
with these ribbons.

MATERIALS AND TOOLS

Assorted cupcake liners
Scissors
White glue
Gift bows
Construction paper
Safety pin (optional)
Double-sided tape (optional)

INSTRUCTIONS

1. Flatten a small cupcake liner. If desired, cut about ½ inch (1.3 cm) off the rim, all the way around the liner. If enough of the larger liner (see step 2) shows around the rim of this liner, don't cut it.

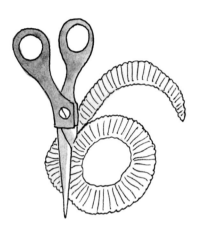

2. Flatten a larger liner and add a drop of glue to the center. Press the smaller liner on top of the larger one. Allow the glue to dry and then flip over the liners so the back is facing up.

3. Cut out paper "ribbons" approximately 5 x ¾ inches (12.7 x 2 cm) from a piece of 5 x 3½-inch (12.7 x 9 cm) construction paper. Cut out a V shape. Holding the V upside down, snip little triangles out of the ends.

4. Apply a dab of glue to the top end of the ribbons, and attach it to the back of the bottom cupcake liner. Let dry.

5. Turn the liners over so the front is face up. Peel the backing off the sticky tab on the bottom of a gift bow and stick the bow in the center of the smaller liner. Glue on a small safety pin or use double-sided tape to attach it to a lapel or gift.

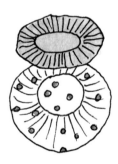

Kajsa Kinsella
INFINITY STONES

Travel through space on a galactic journey with these funky pebbles.

MATERIALS AND TOOLS

Smooth, flat beach stones
Green paint
Black paint
Glow-in-the-dark paint
Small, flat paintbrush
Rubber stamps (stars, planets, lightning bolts)
Black permanent ink pad
Newspapers or plastic

INSTRUCTIONS

1. Wash the stones thoroughly in warm water to get rid of all the sand and salt and let them dry completely before painting.

2. Cover a work surface with newspapers or plastic. Paint some of the stones green and some black and let them dry; each side will need two coats.

3. Paint the green stones with glow-in-the-dark paint all over one side and let them dry. Then check them at night to see if they need another coat of glow-in-the-dark paint.

4. Using the permanent black ink pad, decorate the green stones with rubber-stamp stars, planets, and lightning bolts.

5. Decorate the black stones by stamping them with glow-in-the-dark paint. Paint a little glow-in-the-dark paint onto the stamps before pressing the stamps onto the stones—just enough to make the stamp picture show. Be sure to stamp a rocket ship or two for the journey to the infinite and beyond!

6. Let all the ink and paint dry completely before handling.

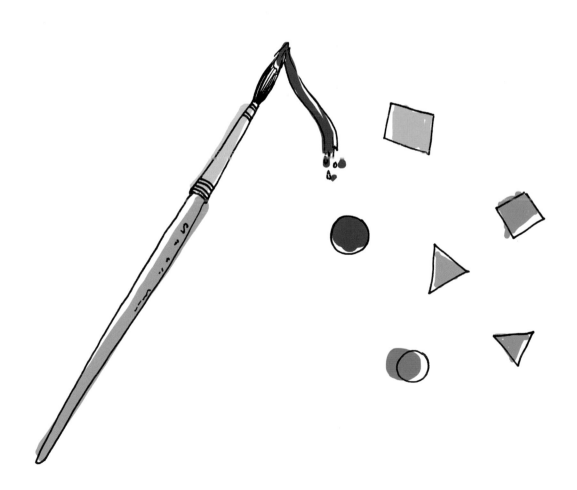

Dora Moreland
PENCIL CAN ORGANIZER

Fill these crafty organizers with sharpened pencils, pens, small rulers, and even scissors, and be ready for homework and other projects!

MATERIALS AND TOOLS

1 empty aluminum can, washed clean and dried completely
1 roll of jute or string
Mod Podge
Several paintbrushes in a variety of sizes
Foam brush
2-3 acrylic paints in a variety of colors
Several cotton swabs
Scissors
Newspaper or plastic to cover work surface

INSTRUCTIONS

1. Paint a stripe of Mod Podge on the can, starting at the bottom edge.

2. Start wrapping jute around the can. Brush more Mod Podge on the end of the jute to secure it well and prevent fraying.

3. After a few rounds, push the wrapped jute closer together and brush more Mod Podge on the can. Make sure the jute is even, smooth, and doesn't overlap.

4. Repeat until the jute reaches the top edge of the can.

5. At the top, cut the jute rope and brush Mod Podge on the end to secure it to the can and prevent fraying.

6. Pick 2–3 colors and, using a brush for each color, paint the jute in stripes.

TIP

Using simple designs is best because painting details on jute can be difficult. Just add bright colors.

7. Use liberal amounts of paint, because the jute will soak it up. Paint over each color again to make it brighter.

8. For dots, use cotton swabs dipped in paint. Make any design.

9. Allow the paints to dry completely.

Karin Schaefer

VOTIVE CANDLE PLATES

CRAFT 1

After a makeover, give your used jam- and jelly-jar lids a second life as as plates for battery-operated votive candles.

MATERIALS AND TOOLS

Metal lids
Acrylic paint
Paintbrush
Glue
Ribbons and lace
Sequins
Battery-operated votive candles
Newspapers or plastic

INSTRUCTIONS

1. Clean and dry the metal lids thoroughly.

2. Cover the work surface with newspapers or plastic to protect it.

3. Paint the lids inside and out with acrylic paint.

TIP

The lids may require more than one coat of paint before they are completely covered.

4. Let the lids dry thoroughly and then glue on ribbons or lace.

5. Glue a small sequin onto the inside bottom of the lid. Make sure the sequin is glued flat to the bottom, or the candle will be unstable.

Karin Schaefer
EMBROIDERED BOTTLES*

Embroidery on plastic—does it really work? Absolutely! Just keep it simple and voilá, a pretty, embroidered bottle to organize your desk! This is also a great way to recycle plastic.

MATERIALS AND TOOLS

2 soft plastic bottles
Scissors
Tape measure
Pencil
Small, single-hole puncher
Needle
Scrap yarn

*This project requires adult supervision.

INSTRUCTIONS

1. Using scissors, cut the bottles to the height needed to hold the desk accessories. Ask an adult for help with this step.

2. Measure the diameter of the bottle and mark where to punch holes. The tops of the holes should be about ½ inch (1.3 cm) below the top edge. Mark an even number of holes and align them all around the bottle.

3. Punch evenly spaced holes on the marks.

4. With a needle, weave the yarn into the punched holes. Start on the outside of the first hole and weave inward if a bow on the outside of the bottle is desired. Start on the inside of the first hole and weave outward if the knot is to be hidden.

5. When finished, tie the ends of the yarn together inside or in a bow on the outside. Trim the ends.

TIP

Use any kind of pattern you like. Try circles, triangles, or even squares. Let your imagination run wild!

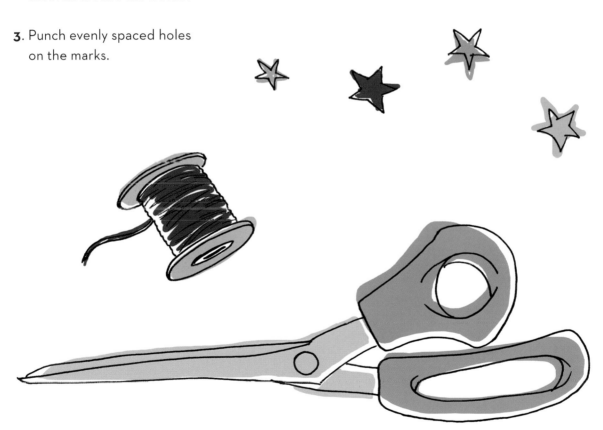

Kajsa Kinsella
WINTER MEMORY GAME

Get the family around the dinner table and play a lovely memory game during those long winter evenings!

MATERIALS AND TOOLS

Terra cotta-colored air-drying clay
Rolling pin
Small cookie cutter, round, square, rectangle, or triangle
Disposable nail file
Red ink pad
Small rubber stamps
Water-based varnish
Newspaper or plastic

INSTRUCTIONS

1. Cover the work surface. Roll the clay out to about ⅛-inch (0.3 cm) thick and press out as many pairs of game parts as needed.

2. Place the pieces on a flat surface in a warm place and let dry for a few days. Turn them over twice a day to speed up the drying process and to keep them flat.

3. When they are dry, the clay pieces will have rough edges that will need to be rubbed off. Use a disposable nail file and work outside, if possible, because this is a fairly dusty job.

4. With a rubber stamp, print a pretty design on one side of the game pieces in bright red ink. Be sure to make an identical pair of each design. Make plenty of pairs in the same shape, but remember to use different designs on them, as one pair is needed for each design.

5. Brush water-based varnish on the top and edges of the game pieces to keep them shiny and clean. When they are dry, turn them over and varnish the other side. Be sure to use water based varnish, because it dries very quickly and does not stay sticky, unlike some kinds of varnish. Give each side a coat or two. Let dry thoroughly between coats.

How to Play

Place all the game pieces face down on a table and take turns turning two over at a time. The player who finds a pair gets to keep it. That player keeps turning over pairs until no match is made. Then the next player turns over pairs until no match is made. When all the pieces have been removed, the player with the most pairs is the winner.

TIP

To make the game a little trickier, stamp with other colors of ink, but use the same designs—it will really test your memory!

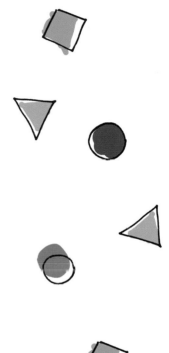

41

Esther Coombs

DOG BOWL AND DAD'S MUG*

CRAFT 2

S tart your own ceramic studio with these cute projects that are sure to put all members of the family in a happy mood—four-legged included.

MATERIALS AND TOOLS

Mug or dog bowl
Templates (see pg. 124)
Pencil
Thick card stock for tracing templates
Scissors
Masking tape
Glass cleaner or soapy water
Fine-tip ceramic marker
Scrap paper
Old cloth
Cotton swabs
Oven

*This project requires adult supervision.

INSTRUCTIONS

1. Before starting these two projects, pick out plain, simple shapes with basic lines and avoid patterns. Drawings will not appear clearly on very dark mugs or bowls, so stick to light-colored pieces.

2. Pick plain and simple mugs as well. Make sure not to pick any new or second-hand ones with chips, cracks, or crackle in the glaze.

3. The bowl or mug needs to be very clean. Clean it thoroughly by running it through the dishwasher on a hot cycle or by hand washing in hot water. (Ask an adult for help with this if necessary). The hot wash will show that the pieces will survive the hot conditions of the oven baking at the end of the project. Dry completely.

4. Trace the template design with a pencil onto card stock.

5. Cut out the card stock template and attach it to the mug or bowl with masking tape to hold it in the correct position. (Roll the tape onto itself to form a loop, sticky side out, and pop it onto the back of the template to hold it on the mug or bowl. That way, there will be no tape on the edges of the template to be in the way.)

6. Pump the tip of the marker onto a sheet of scrap paper to make the ink flow smoothly.

TIP

If the ink in the ceramic marker becomes thick and gloppy, dab the nib with a cloth. If the ink flows too slowly, pump the tip, shake the pen, and pump the tip again.

7. When the ink flows well, trace the template on scrap paper a few times before trying it on the mug or bowl. Hold the mug or bowl comfortably in one hand for drawing. Using the ceramic marker, trace around the edge of the template onto the mug or bowl. Follow the edges closely, keeping the lines steady and even.

8. Once the design has been completely traced, let the mug or bowl dry for 10 minutes.

9. Peel off the template and masking tape and repeat the template design in several places on the mug or bowl, if desired.

TIP

If the tracing did not come out well, wipe it off with glass cleaner or soapy water and an old cloth. A cotton swab is a great tool for tidying up any small mistakes.

10. Once the tracings are finished, set aside and allow to dry for 24 hours, or until fully dry.

11. Ask an adult to place the mug or bowl into a cold oven and then set the oven temperature to 300ºF (150ºC). Once the oven has reached the temperature, allow the mug or bowl to bake for 35 minutes.

12. Once the baking is finished, ask an adult to turn off the oven. Leave the oven door slightly ajar until the mug or bowl has slowly cooled completely. This will take a while, so be patient to see the finished product!

Jane Bailey Kohlenstein

APPLIQUÉD FLEECE SCARF*

The cold weather never felt so warm as with these stylish scarves, which also make for a great gift idea.

MATERIALS AND TOOLS

¼ yard of fleece (9 inches; 22 cm)
Felt
Buttons
Coordinating embroidery floss
   or thread
Scissors
Straight pins
Sewing Machine (optional)
Two rulers
Templates (see pg. 125–127)

INSTRUCTIONS

1. Cut a long rectangle of fleece ¼ yard (9 inches; 22 cm) long and the width of the fabric, typically about 58–62 inches (147–157 cm).

TIP

Before beginning the design, try on the fleece to see if it needs to be shortened. A younger child may want a scarf closer to 50 inches (127 cm) long, rather than one that is 60 inches (152 cm).

2. Choose an appliqué pattern template (see page 125–127) and cut out the coordinating pieces of felt using the pattern pieces.

3. Pin each design into place approximately 6 inches (15 cm) up from the bottom edge, using the pattern diagram as a guide for placement. Once the felt pieces are pinned, carefully begin to sew them onto the scarf. There are two different ways to sew the appliqués in place. Option 1: With the help of an adult, use a sewing machine and simply stitch around the edges of the felt pieces. Option 2: Stitch around the edges with embroidery floss using a running stitch.

TIP

A running stitch is a simple, straight stitch made by repeatedly pushing the needle in and out of the fabric with short, even stitches and no overlapping. The stitches should look like this: - - - - - - - - - - - .

4. For the fox, raccoon, and mouse faces, stitch the face pieces onto the fleece first. Then add buttons for the eyes and nose. Finally, stitch the entire face to the fleece. (You can also stitch the faces directly onto the fleece right at the beginning.)

5. Now, it's time to fringe the scarf. Fold the scarf in half, aligning the two short ends together. Lay a ruler across the scarf about 4 inches (10 cm) from the bottom to use as a guide and cut a ½-inch (1.3 cm) wide strip through both ends of the scarf simultaneously. Stop cutting at the ruler. Be careful not to cut too close or through the appliqué! Continue cutting strips all the way across the ends of the scarf, making 4-inch (10 cm) long cuts about every ½ inch (1.3 cm).

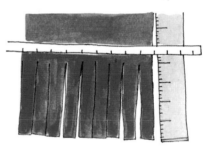

Cynthia Shaffer

PAPER CLIP AND TAPE NECKLACES*

CRAFT

2

Move over boring gray duct tape and make way for the new! Transform this quick, go-to fixer into a chic and modern accessory.

MATERIALS AND TOOLS

Black, White, and Green-Print Necklace
Black, white, and green-print duct tape
69 silver paper clips, 1¼ inches (3.2 cm)
Self-healing craft mat
Pencil
Ruler
Craft knife

Orange, White, and Orange-Print Necklace
Orange, white, and orange-print
   duct tape
36 silver paper clips, 1¼ inches (3.2 cm)
Self-healing craft mat
Pencil
Ruler
Craft knife

*This project requires adult supervision.

BLACK, WHITE, AND GREEN-PRINT NECKLACE

INSTRUCTIONS

1. Affix the black duct tape to the craft mat. Use the pencil and ruler to draw 20 pieces 2½ x ¾ inches (6.35 x 1.9 cm) wide. Cut each piece with the craft knife and leave them on the mat until they are needed. Ask an adult for help with this step.

TIP

Duct tape is available in different widths. The black and white tape used for this necklace measured 2 inches (5 cm) wide and had to be cut to ¾ inch (1.9 cm).

2. Wrap one piece of tape around one paper clip, leaving a ¼-inch (0.6-cm) space at each end.

3. Hook another paper clip onto the end of this wrapped clip and repeat steps 2 and 3 until the chain is 20 paper clips long. Set aside.

4. Repeat steps 1–3 for the white duct tape until the chain is 23 paper clips long.

5. Repeat steps 1–3 for the green print duct tape until the chain is 25 paper clips long.

6. Hook one unwrapped paper clip to the 6 ends of the chains and then wrap the last paper clip with a length of white duct tape. Now this pretty necklace can be worn with style!

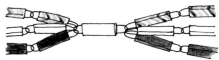

ORANGE, WHITE, AND ORANGE-PRINT NECKLACE

INSTRUCTIONS

1. Stick the orange-print duct tape to the craft mat. Use the pencil and ruler to draw 30 pieces each 2½-inches (6.35 cm) long and ¾-inch (1.9 cm) wide. Cut each piece with the craft knife and leave them on the mat until they are needed. Ask an adult for help with this step.

TIP

Duct tape is available in different widths. The orange and white tape used for this necklace measured 1¾ inches (4.4 cm) wide and was cut to ¾ inch (1.9 cm). The orange print tape measured ¾ inch (1.9 cm) and did not need to be cut down.

2. Wrap one piece of tape around one paper clip, leaving a ¼-inch (0.6-cm) space at each end.

3. Hook another paper clip onto the end of this wrapped clip and repeat steps 2 and 3 until the chain is 23 paper clips long.

4. Hook one paper clip through the wrapped paper clips at each end of the chain to make a complete loop. Wrap this paper clip with a cut length of duct tape.

5. Find the center of the necklace where two paper clips are hooked. This is where a pendant will hang. Hook two paper clips into the end of one of those paper clips. Wrap these two paper clips with orange tape.

6. Spread these two new paper clips into a V shape and hook another clip into the hanging ends so it is horizontal and creates a triangle. Wrap the paper clip with orange tape.

7. Hook one paper clip from each end of this paper clip. Wrap these paper clips with white tape.

8. Hook one paper clip horizontally into the end of these two hanging paper clips to make a square. Wrap this paper clip with white tape.

9. Hook three paper clips into the each corner of the bottom of the square. Wrap these six paper clips with the orange-print duct tape.

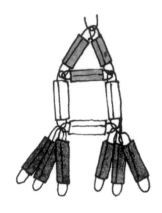

Sarah Olmsted

BIRD TOSS ORNITHOLOGY GAME*

CRAFT

2

Toss out the horseshoes and try this fun game at your next gathering at the beach, lake, park, or even your backyard!

MATERIALS AND TOOLS

- Bird reference guide (optional)
- Bird silhouette templates (*see pg. 128–132*)
- Scrap fabric in different patterns and/or colors
- 24 x 24 inch (61 x 61 cm) piece of canvas
- Needle (or sewing machine) and thread in complementary colors
- 2 lb (1 kg) bag of rice or lentils (for filling the bags)
- Fabric paint (3 or more colors)
- Paper
- Pencil
- Paintbrush
- Funnel (optional)
- Bamboo skewer or chopstick (optional)
- Small cloth bag or tote (optional)

*This project requires adult supervision.

INSTRUCTIONS

1. Copy the bird silhouette patterns (see page 128–132) and then cut out the paper shapes with scissors. As an alternative, look through bird guides and draw silhouettes freehand, making sure your drawings are roughly the same size as the bird templates.

2. Trace the shapes of the paper templates onto fabric that is folded over. For a patterned fabric, make sure the right sides of the fabric are together before cutting. Cut out each shape, leaving about ¼ inch (6 mm) of fabric outside the line. Sew along the line, leaving about a 1¼-inch (3.2 cm) gap open along a straight side near the bottom of the bird shape.

3. Before turning the birds right-side out, cut small V notches in the cloth outside the seam (making sure not to cut the stitches) wherever the pattern curves greatly. This will keep the fabric from pulling.

4. To get the narrow parts turned out, it may help to use a bamboo skewer or chopstick. Once the bird is turned right-side out, fill it

with rice or lentils and sew up the openings securely. (You're going to be throwing the birds at a target, so stitch the openings very well, so they don't open.) Use a blanket stitch to do this, if possible. You can add a tag with the bird's name, embroider the name directly on the bottom of the bird, or write it with a fabric marker, if you wish.

5. To make the "bird's nest" target, lightly sketch three rings of "branches" with a pencil on the 24 x 24 inch (61 x 61 cm) piece of canvas. Don't worry about making the rings perfectly round; any bumps or lumps will look beautiful. Starting with the biggest ring, paint in the outline with fabric paint. Next, in a different color, paint the middle ring, and finally the center ring. Allow the fabric paint to dry for 24 hours.

6. Once the paint is dry, set the colors by ironing the target for 30 seconds on each side of the fabric. Ask an adult for help with this if you are new to using an iron. Run a zigzag stitch around the edges of the canvas to keep it from fraying. Ask an adult for help if you are using a sewing machine.

7. To make an optional carrying case for the game, purchase a solid-colored cloth bag or tote (often available at craft stores) and use the paper templates and fabric paint to stencil a bird silhouette on the bag. Allow to dry for 24 hours and set with an iron before using.

TIP

Take this opportunity to learn a little more about Earth's feathered friends in a bird reference guide.

To Play the Game

1. Instruct each player to select a bird beanbag.

2. Ask them to (one by one) try their hand at tossing the beanbags onto the target.

3. Assign point values to each ring and keep track of how many points each player has.

4. After 4-8 rounds, tally the points to select the winner.

BONUS POINTS

Players can earn bonus points by sharing facts they know about birds during each round.

Amber Dohrenwend

PULP
NECKLACE*

CRAFT 2

What to do with those old egg cartons? Pulp them and create jewelry!

MATERIALS AND TOOLS

4-5 paper egg cartons
1 C (240 ml) measuring cup
Water
Blender or immersion blender
Colander or sieve
Large bowl
Large paper clip
Towel or drying rack
Oven, dehydrator, or a dry, sunny spot
Watercolor paints
Small craft paintbrush
Yarn, ribbon, or string cut to the
    desired length, plus extra for tying
    the ends into a bow

*This project requires adult supervision.

INSTRUCTIONS

1. Tear up the egg cartons into coin-size pieces and place them in a large bowl. Cover with water and let soak overnight.

2. With the help of an adult, combine 1 cup of soaked, well-packed, egg carton pieces and 6 cups (1.43 L) water in a blender (or a bowl, if using an immersion blender). Mix until pulp is the consistency of smooth oatmeal. Repeat the process 3-4 times, until all pulp is used.

3. Pour the mixture into a colander or sieve and allow to drain for a few minutes.

4. When the mixture begins to look lumpy, take a portion the size of a golf ball and gently squeeze it to get more of the water out. Working carefully, gently shape the paper pulp into the desired bead shapes. Round, square, and triangular shapes work best. Don't squeeze out too much water while forming the beads. They dry the strongest when a little moisture is left in them.

5. If the beads begin to crumble or fall apart during shaping, return them to the pulp mixture, add some more water, drain, and begin again.

6. Once a bead is formed, gently make a hole through the center with a straightened paper clip.

7. Place the finished beads on a towel or drying rack.

8. Allow them to dry in a sunny spot until they become extremely hard. It may take a few days, depending on the amount of sun and temperature. With the help of an adult, use a dehydrator to dry them, or an oven set to 250°F (120°C) for 2 to 3 hours.

9. Use vivid watercolors to decorate the beads in different colors and patterns.

10. String the beads on colored yarn, ribbon, or string and tie the ends into a bow.

VARIATION

Instead of a necklace, try making matching bracelets, too, for a complete pulp look!

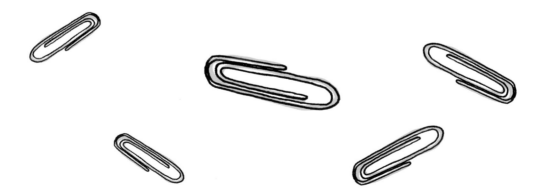

Dora Moreland
CHECKERS AND CHECKERBOARD BAG

CRAFT
2

Looking for a modern twist on checkers? This felt version is not only the colorful answer, but is also portable!

MATERIALS AND TOOLS

3 felt sheets, 9 x 12 (23 x 30.5 cm) each (two in one color and one in a contrasting color)
24 wooden circles, 1-inch (2.5 cm) diameter
Yarn, string, ribbon
2 beads
Ruler
Pencil
Scissors
Felt glue
Embroidery thread to match the color of the two matching pieces of felt
Embroidery needle
Single-hole punch
Paintbrush
2 acrylic paints, in different colors
Fine-tipped marker

53

INSTRUCTIONS

To Construct the Checkerboard Bag

1. Using a ruler and pencil, measure and mark thirty two 1-inch (2.5 cm) squares on the contrasting color felt sheet. The easiest way to do this is to draw 1-inch (2.5 cm) wide strips and then divide the strips into 1-inch (2.5 cm) squares. Cut the squares from the fabric.

2. Arrange squares in a checkerboard pattern so the corners just meet on one of the other color sheets of felt. Glue them well with the felt glue. Be sure all the edges and corners are glued firmly to the background felt.

3. Thread the embroidery needle with the floss.

4. Place second felt sheet onto the back of the first. Push the needle into a corner all the way through both layers of felt. Sew around three sides with a running stitch, leaving the top open to make a bag. Finish with a square knot.

TIP

Hide the knots between the layers of felt when you start and finish sewing. A running stitch looks like this - - - - -.

5. Using a ruler and pencil, make dots on the front and back of felt at the open top of the bag about 1–2 inches (2.5–5 cm) below the top and about 1 inch (2.5 cm) apart. Punch holes with the hole punch at each dot. Make sure the holes are evenly spaced and aligned and end at an even number.

6. Insert a ribbon or string through one of the front center holes from the outside to the inside of the bag. Weave it all around the bag to end at the hole next to the starting hole. Add a bead to the ends of the ribbon and tie a knot on each end to keep the beads in place.

To Construct the Checkers

1. Divide the wooden circles into two sets of 12.

2. Paint one set one color or design and the other a different one. See below for designs. Allow them to dry completely.

3. Using a marker, draw crowns on one side of all the wooden circles.

4. After the checkers are all painted and decorated, store them in the checkerboard bag for a game ready to go anywhere, anytime!

 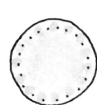

Trice Boerens
MINI PIÑATAS*

Nothing says "¡Viva la fiesta!" like these cheerful piñatas that are great for birthdays, parties, or even backyard barbeques.

MATERIALS AND TOOLS

2 small paper cups
Candy
5-inch (12.7 cm) long pipe cleaner
8-inch (20.3 cm) long paper twist
Large needle
Fine wire or thread
Double-sided tape or adhesive
2 colors of tissue paper
Scissors

*This project requires adult supervision.

INSTRUCTIONS

1. Turn a cup upside down and mark the center of the bottom.

2. With a needle, carefully punch a hole through mark. Ask an adult to help.

3. Form a loop with the pipe cleaner and thread the paper twist through the loop.

4. Wrap the neck of the paper twist with the wire or thread, and twist or tie to secure it.

5. Slide both ends of the pipe cleaner through the cup hole and twist. Open the ends to form a V shape.

6. Line the rim of the top cup with double-sided tape. Set aside.

7. Fill the bottom cup with candy. Align the two cups at the rims and press them firmly together.

8. From the tissue paper, cut several 1 x 8-inch (2.5 x 20 cm) strips. Make perpendicular cuts in strips to make the fringe.

9. Wrap the cups with the double-sided tape. Make sure to cover the top and bottom edges.

10. Starting at the bottom edge, apply a fringe strip to the cup in a spiral pattern. Overlap and trim the ends.

11. Apply a second row of fringe that slightly overlaps the first row until the entire

piece is covered. Cut more fringe strips as needed, and add rows until the piece is completely covered.

12. Wrap a solid strip of tissue paper around the top and bottom edges to cover the spiral ends and give the final piece a finished look

13. Carefully unwind both sides of the paper twist, and cut the ends to make streamers. Trim the ends.

TIP

Paper twists can be purchased in a variety of colors and sizes at craft stores.

Chiara Alberetti Milott

STRAW GARLAND

CRAFT

2

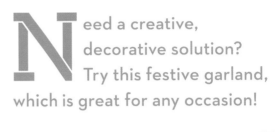

Need a creative, decorative solution? Try this festive garland, which is great for any occasion!

MATERIALS AND TOOLS

Assorted cupcake liners
Scissors
Card stock in various colors
1-inch (2.5 cm) diameter hole punch or scissors
Regular hole punch
Twine
Assorted striped paper straws.

INSTRUCTIONS

1. Punch out (or cut out) a few 1-inch (2.5 cm) circles from card stock, and punch a small hole in the center of each circle. (The number needed depends on the length of the garland.)

2. Cut a small hole in the bottom center of the cupcake liners.

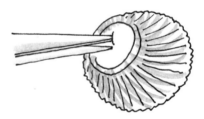

3. Cut paper straws into 3- and 4-inch (7.5 and 10 cm) lengths.

4. Knot the end of the twine, and thread the twine through a straw.

5. Thread the twine through a 1-inch (2.5 cm) dot, then a cupcake liner, then another 1-inch (2.5 cm) dot, and another piece of straw. When using a number of straws in a row, slip a dot between each one, because the 1-inch (2.5 cm) dot prevents the cupcake liners and straws from slipping over one another.

6. Repeat step 5, switching the direction of the cupcake liners, until you reach the desired garland length. Knot the end of the twine.

TIP

To add twine while working, tie a square knot tightly and trim the ends. Try to hide the knot inside one of the straws.

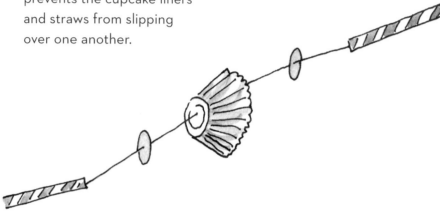

Karin Schaefer
DENIM BASKET

CRAFT **2**

A lmost anything can be up-cycled—even worn-out pants—and used again.

MATERIALS AND TOOLS

Old, worn-out, straight-legged jeans
  or denim pants
Scissors
Thread
Needle
Buttons, ribbons, and other notions

INSTRUCTIONS

1. Measuring from the bottom seam, cut a piece of the pants leg about 8 inches (20 cm) long. Keep the original bottom seam.

2. Sew the cut edge together with the right sides facing each other. This will become the bottom of the basket.

3. Sew a diagonal line across each corner to create two triangles on both ends of the seam.

4. Turn the basket right side out and fold down the top to make it more stable.

5. Decorate the folded-down top cuff with ribbons and buttons or other notions.

TIP

At your next gathering, fill these baskets with party favors instead of using plastic ones!

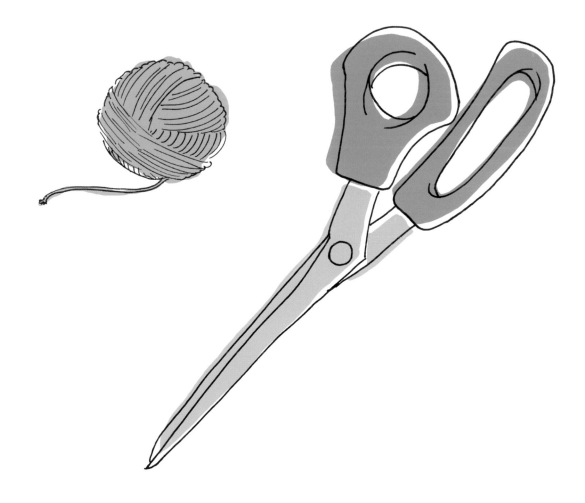

John Murphy
STICKER BOMBS*

CRAFT
2

Cover household items with cartoon faces to give them life . . . or to play a prank.

MATERIALS AND TOOLS

Photocopier
Full-sheet label paper or standard
   copy paper
Markers
Scissors or craft knife
Self-healing craft mat
Glue stick (optional, but use with the
   standard copy paper)
Template (see pg. 134–135)

*This project requires adult supervision.

INSTRUCTIONS

TIP

*Check that surfaces will not
be damaged when applying
the stickers.*

1. Photocopy the page of
   cartoon face parts onto
   full-sheet label paper or
   onto standard copier paper.

2. Use markers to color the
   pictures or alter the designs.

3. Using scissors or a craft
   knife, cut out the images
   carefully. Ask an adult for
   help if needed.

4. Peel off the backing of
   the label paper or apply
   a glue stick to the back
   of the image.

5. Toon-faces can be stuck on
   anything they won't harm.

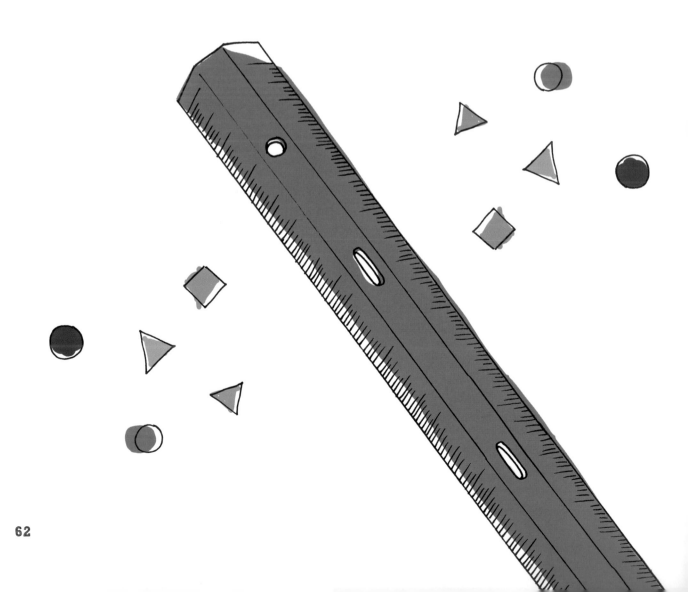

Cynthia Shaffer
MACRAMÉ BRACELET

Show your friendship with this unique bracelet, which is a fun alternative to the traditional version!

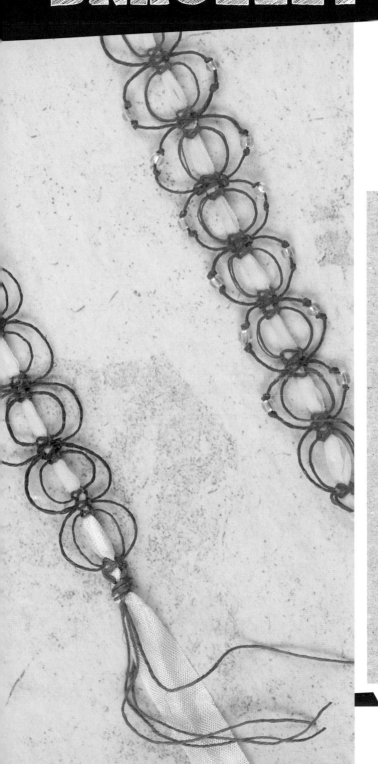

MATERIALS AND TOOLS

Blue Bracelet
5 yards (4.6 m) of blue hemp cording
15 inches (38 cm) of ½-inch (1.3 cm) wide ribbon

Pink-and-Orange Bracelet
2½ yards (2.3 m) pink hemp cording
2½ yards (2.3 m) orange hemp cording
16 clear beads (4 mm wide, 1½ mm hole)
15 inches (38 cm) of 12-inch (1.3-cm) wide ribbon

For Both Bracelets
Paper
Pencil
Ruler
Clipboard
2 Tbs. (30 mL) craft glue
1 Tbs. (15 mL) water
Small mixing bowl
Measuring spoon
Mixing spoon
Plastic sheet, 8 x 10 inches (20.3 x 25.4 cm)
Craft paintbrush

BLUE BRACELET

INSTRUCTIONS

1. Mark a 6-inch (15.24 cm) straight line lengthwise on the paper. Mark the beginning of the line, the middle, and the end of the line. Attach this paper to the clipboard and use the line as a guide to know how long to make the bracelet.

2. Cut four lengths of hemp 40 inches (1 m) long.

3. Cut one length of ribbon 15 inches (38 cm) long.

4. Knot the hemp and the ribbon together, leaving about a 4-inch (10 cm) tail.

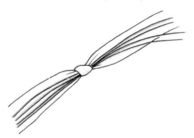

5. Using all four strands of hemp, two on each side of the ribbon, form a square knot around the ribbon.

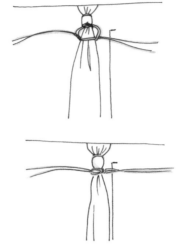

6. Using just the inner two lengths of hemp (one piece from right next to each side of the ribbon) form a square knot around the ribbon.

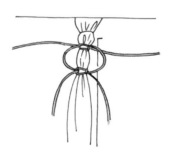

7. Now, using only the outer hemp lengths, form a square knot around both the ribbon and the inner hemp lengths.

8. Form a square knot with the inner hemp lengths around the ribbon.

TIP

When forming the knots to make this bracelet, allow the cording to bow out a bit and then pull the knots tightly closed around the ribbon. Allow them to lie flat against the paper. Keep all the knots uniform in size.

9. Repeat steps 5 and 8 until you reach the 6-inch (15 cm) line on your paper.

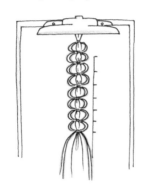

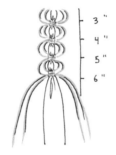

10. Form a square knot using all four lengths of hemp. Make sure the hemp on each side of the inner ribbon is still flat before pulling the knot snug.

11. Knot the ribbon and the hemp together, as was done in step 4.

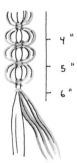

12. Trim the remaining ribbon and hemp to 4 inches (10 cm).

13. Mix together the water and the white craft glue in a small bowl.

14. Place the bracelet on the plastic. With a paintbrush, apply the glue mixture only to the knotted portion of the bracelet.

15. Allow the bracelet to dry.

16. Wrap the bracelet around your wrist and tie the ends together.

PINK-AND-ORANGE BRACELET

INSTRUCTIONS

1. Follow steps 1-5 of the blue bracelet. After step 5, knot the outer strand of hemp and then thread it onto a small bead. Push the bead up to the knot and then form another knot to keep the bead from slipping. Repeat for the other outer hemp cord and then move on to step 6.

2. Arrange the hemp cord so that the pink strands are on the outside and the orange strands are inside next to the ribbon.

3. Using just the inner two orange lengths of hemp, form a square knot around the ribbon.

4. Knot the outer pink strand of hemp to keep the bead from slipping. Push the bead up to the knot and then form another knot to keep the bead from slipping. Repeat for the other outer pink hemp cord.

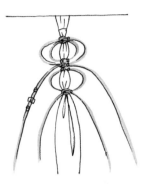

5. Repeat steps 5 and 8 until you reach the 6-inch (15 cm) line on your paper.

6. Repeat steps 10-16 of the blue bracelet.

Chiara Alberetti Milott

CARDBOARD PLAYHOUSE

CRAFT **2**

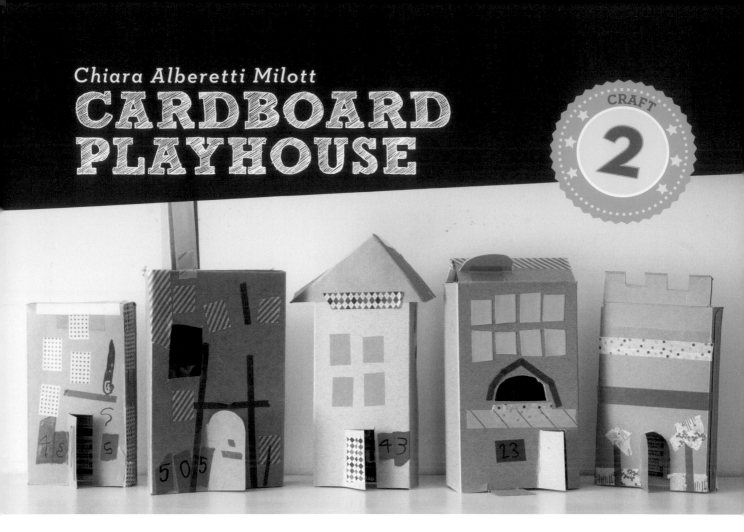

As they say, "It takes a village," so gather your family citizens together to make this fun project.

MATERIALS AND TOOLS

Leftover grocery boxes (mac-and-cheese boxes are the perfect size, but cereal boxes work too.)
Scissors
Assorted decorative washi tapes
Markers

INSTRUCTIONS

1. Begin by turning the box upside down and cutting from the open top along one long edge. At the bottom of the box, turn the scissors 90 degrees and cut along the short edge, then turn the scissors again and cut the next bottom edge. Finally, cut the other short edge.

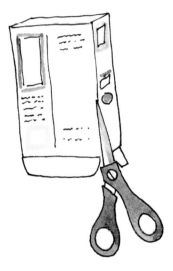

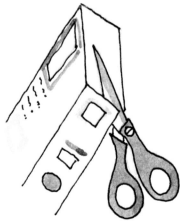

2. There is now a flap, so fold this flap back.

3. Flatten the box and cut off the top of the box completely (the edge that had originally been opened to remove the food).

4. Turn the box inside out and tape the two long edges together.

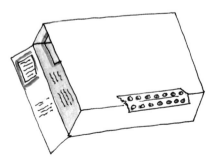

5. Fold the flap down again and tape it closed.

6. Cut a small door by cutting a "7" into one of the larger sides of the box and then bending the door open. Cut out windows.

7. Use washi tape and markers to embellish and decorate the house.

8. Get creative and add chimneys, slanted roofs, window boxes. Put houses together to make a village.

TIP

For extra embellishments, use stickers, pom-poms, buttons, sequins, beads, or anything you can find. Be creative!

Jane Bailey Kohlenstein

EGG CUP-FLOWER MOBILE*

Try this great and stylish mobile to reuse your old egg boxes.

MATERIALS AND TOOLS

2 or 3 one-dozen cardboard egg cartons
Scissors
Watercolors
Paintbrush
Tapestry needle
Butcher's twine or plain white string
Stick
Newspapers or plastic

*This project requires adult supervision.

INSTRUCTIONS

1. Begin by cutting the cardboard egg cartons: Cut off and discard the top of the egg carton, saving only the bottom part (where the eggs rest). With help from an adult, very carefully cut across the carton from front to back and remove two egg cups at a time. Repeat five times, so there are six egg cup pairs. Carefully cut across the pairs to make single egg cups. Hold a cup in one hand and use the other to cut out a triangle from each of its four sides, so the corners of the cups look like flower petals. Do this for the other eleven cups. Repeat for the other cardboard egg cartons being used.

2. After all the cardboard flowers have been cut, paint them with watercolors. Be sure to cover the work surface first with newspapers or plastic. Paint both the inside and the outside of each cup, because both will be visible on the mobile. Paint them with different colored stripes or dots, all one color, one color on the inside and another on the outside, or randomly—with no plan at all. Have fun with it!

3. While the flowers are still a bit wet with paint, gently pull the petals outward to make them flair a little. Allow the egg cups to dry with the petals facing down. The drying time will vary depending on how much paint is used, but it's good to leave them overnight.

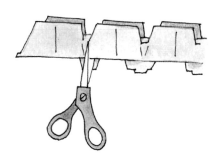

4. With help from an adult, thread the butcher's twine or string through a tapestry needle. Tie a knot at the end of the twine and carefully, from inside the eggcup, push the needle through the center of the cup base. The tapestry needle has a blunt tip, which makes it safer to use; but be very careful anyway!

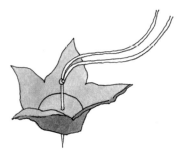

TIP

Because a tapestry needle has a blunt tip, it will require some pressure to poke through the bottom of the flower cup. Try placing the eye of the needle (the back end of it) onto a hard surface—but not on a piece of furniture that could show nicks and dents—and pressing the inside of the cup base onto the tip to help poke the needle through. Ask an adult to help with this step.

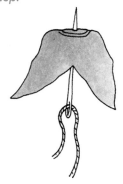

5. Once the twine is pulled all the way through one flower cup, tie another knot about 2 inches (5 cm) from the cup. Add the next flower. Continue in this manner to create a chain of flowers on the twine.

6. String as many flowers as desired on one piece of twine. Then start another of a different length. Repeat until all the flowers have been strung on different lengths of twine. Vary the flower colors and designs.

7. Tie each different length to the stick with the end of twine used to make the strings. Hang and enjoy the beautiful flower mobile!

TIP

Use a screw hook (or eye) screwed into the ceiling. Tie two lengths of butcher's twine (or string) near each end of the stick, bring the two lengths together above the mobile, and tie them together about 4 inches (10 cm) from the ends to form a string "triangle" above the mobile. Feed the untied ends through the screw eye (or hook) and bring the ends back to the string "triangle" to tie together in a knot.

Ashley Little

GALAXY T-SHIRT

Use a few bottles of fabric spray paint to create galaxies and stars. There's no wrong way to paint this shirt, and each one looks completely different from any others.

MATERIALS AND TOOLS

1 solid black T-shirt
3 Tulip Fabric Spray Paints—1 each in
  Sapphire, Grape, and Snow
Newspapers or plastic
Cardboard that's very slightly smaller
  than width and height of the T-shirt
Old clothing that can stand up to a
  spray-paint mistake
Rubber gloves

INSTRUCTIONS

1. Cover a work area with newspapers or plastic to protect it. Put on old clothing that's appropriate for painting. Put on rubber gloves to protect your hands.

2. Insert the cardboard inside the shirt to stop the paint from soaking through to the other side.

3. Starting with the Snow spray paint, spritz the shirt in several different places. Keep in mind that the Snow paint is the first layer because it is the background for the other two colors, so don't be shy when spritzing. There's no wrong way to paint this T-shirt!

4. Spray the Grape paint. Spritz randomly, covering some of the Snow paint. Remember that the Grape is a dark color, so the only way it will show up well is if it's sprayed on top of the Snow.

5. Finally, spray the Sapphire paint. If most of the Snow spots were covered with Grape, feel free to add a few more spritzes of Snow and then spray the Sapphire on top of them.

6. Blend wet paints together with a glove-covered finger to create what might be a comet or even a planet!

7. Play around with the design until the galaxy is complete. Add a few final spritzes of Snow to give the galaxy a little bit of light.

8. Let the T-shirt dry overnight. After the front is dry, the T-shirt can be flipped over to make another galaxy on the back!

Suzie Millions

BITTY BEAVER*

CRAFT

3

Feed your curiosity with this cute little critter.

MATERIALS AND TOOLS

- 2 black pipe cleaners
- 3 medium-brown pipe cleaners
- Ruler
- Wire cutters or utility scissors
- Black Sharpie marker
- Toothpick
- Small piece of black felt, alligator pattern if available
- Transparent tape, at least ½-inch (1.3 cm) wide
- Yellow plastic lacing cord, 3 inches (7.6 cm) long
- Sharp scissors to cut felt
- 2 small plastic eyes with stems
- Hot glue (optional)
- 2½-inch (6.4 cm) long narrow twig
- Plastic knife
- Template (see pg. 142)

*This project requires adult supervision.

INSTRUCTIONS

1. For the arms and legs, cut a black pipe cleaner into two 6-inch (15 cm) pieces. Hold the two pieces even next to each other and twist twice in the center. Spread the ends out a little to look like an X. The ends will become the arms and legs.

2. For the head, coil one brown pipe cleaner four times around the end of a black Sharpie marker, starting on the narrower end. Slide it off the pen. The coils will be the head, and the straight piece, about 2 inches (5cm) long, is the backbone.

3. Coil the second brown pipe cleaner to make a flat spiral, like a cinnamon roll. Wrap it around a toothpick first to get

it started and then slide the toothpick out. Hold the flat, round coil up to the back of the head and wrap the short backbone around the long straight piece at the end of the round coil.

4. Tape the template for the tail onto a piece of black felt. Cut it out.

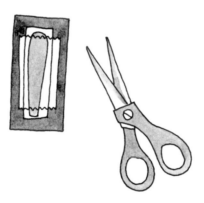

5. Hold the brown head piece behind the black body. Hold the skinny end of the tail just below the arms. Wrap the long straight brown piece tightly around the end of the tail a few times to hold the tail in place. Continue wrapping to make the body until the brown pipe cleaner is completely used.

6. Beavers have a layer of fat under their thick coats so this one needs to be fattened up a little. Make another coil from the third brown pipe cleaner by it wrapping around the black permanent marker. Slide it off. Push the beaver's legs together and slide the brown coil over the feet and tail.

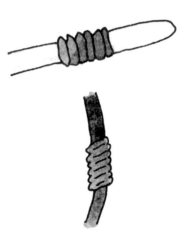

7. Tie a knot in the middle of the piece of yellow plastic lace. Position the knotted plastic lace in the middle of a black pipe cleaner left over from step 1, and wrap the pipe cleaner tightly around the knot three times to form a nose.Trim the ends of the yellow plastic to 1½ inches (3.8 cm) long. Push the ends

of the nose into the narrow end of the face. The yellow lace forms the teeth. Trim the teeth with scissors to ¼-inch (0.6 cm) long.

8. Tape the ear template to the black felt and cut out the ears. Position the piece between the "cinnamon roll" at the back of the head and the rest of the head. With the help of an adult, carefully use the end of the scissors to poke the center of this piece down into the coils to make two ears that spring up a little on the sides.

9. Slide the eye stems between the third and fourth coils on the face. To make them extra secure, ask an adult to put a dot of hot glue behind each one.

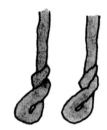

10. Make two bends in the black pipe cleaner on the bottom of the body to make wide flipper feet. Wrap each end once around the straight leg.

11. Scrape a little bark off the middle of the twig with a plastic knife to make it look like the beaver has been snacking. Roll the arms around each end of the stick until the beaver is holding it. Position the stick near its mouth.

TIP

To make this project more accessible for smaller children, an adult could cut the pipe cleaners in advance. Cut out the two felt pieces with the sharp scissors and then break a stick and carve a little notch in the middle of it. To make the eyes more secure, the adult could add a dot of hot glue behind them once the animal has been assembled.

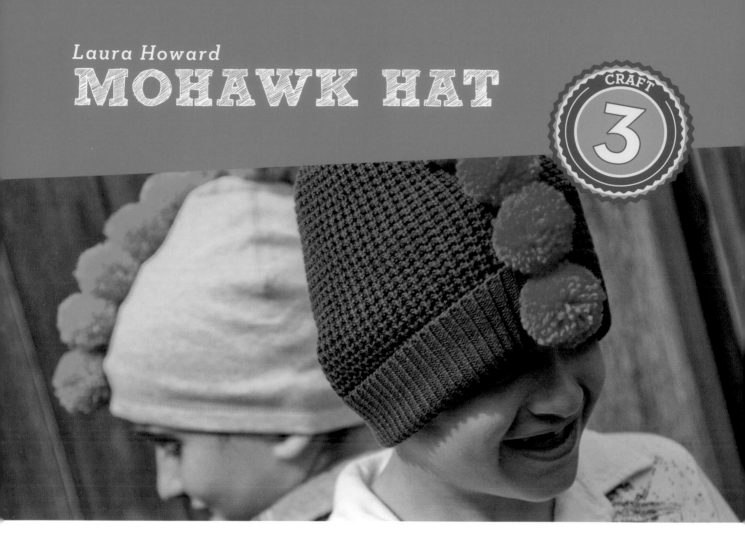

Laura Howard
MOHAWK HAT

CRAFT
3

Turn any ordinary cap into an awesome Mohawk with pom-poms. Follow the instructions to make pom-poms (see page 108) or buy a tool at the craft store to make your own.

MATERIALS AND TOOLS

Scrap cardboard
Compass
Pencil
Scissors for cutting cardboard
Transparent tape
Brightly colored yarn
Sharp sewing or embroidery scissors
   for cutting yarn
Ruler or tape measure
Large, sharp sewing needle
1 knitted, fabric, or fleece cap

INSTRUCTIONS

TIP

The pom-poms pictured were made with DK (double knit) acrylic yarn but any yarn can be used if it's not too thick to sew through the hat. The scrap cardboard is from an empty tissue or cereal box. This thickness is ideal, because the pom-pom–making template needs to be slightly flexible. The sewing needle should be large enough to thread yarn through and sharp enough to sew through the cap.

To Construct the Pom-poms

1. Use the compass to draw a 2-inch (5 cm) diameter circle on the scrap cardboard. Then draw a 3⁄4-inch (2 cm) diameter circle in the center, creating a ring shape. Repeat this step to have 2 rings the same size.

TIP

Want larger pom-poms? Just draw larger circles!

2. Carefully cut out each ring, cutting a straight line through it to access the smaller circles and cutting them out. Use a narrow piece of sticky tape to stick the rings together where they are cut. These two rings are the pom-pom templates.

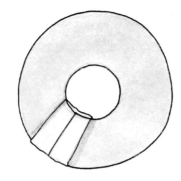

3. Cut six long strands of yarn. The pom-poms pictured were made with six strands of DK yarn 52 inches (132 cm) long, but more or less yarn can be used, depending on how thick it is. Make sure to note how much yarn was used in the first pom-pom so the rest can all be the same size. Also, cut a 20-inch (50 cm) piece of yarn.

4. Place the two pom-pom templates together and gradually wrap the yarn around the cardboard ring, covering it as evenly as possible. Use three strands of the yarn at once to complete this step faster.

5. Hold the yarn-wrapped ring tightly between the thumb and forefingers of one hand.

Use a pair of sharp fabric or embroidery scissors to cut the yarn, cutting around the edge of the ring until there's no more yarn wrapped around it.

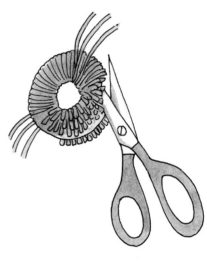

6. Still holding the ring tightly, take the shorter piece of yarn cut in step 3, wrap it around the middle of the pom-pom (in between the two templates) and tie it tightly. This piece of yarn is what holds the pom-pom together, so tie it as tightly as possible and make sure it's knotted securely.

7. Carefully remove the card rings and use scissors to neaten the pom-pom, trimming any excess strands except the two long ends of the yarn that tied the pom-pom together.

8. Repeat steps 3–7 to make lots of pom-poms!

To Decorate the Hat

1. Make approximately thirteen pom-poms—the number used for decorating each hat pictured. More or fewer pom-poms may be needed. if you make more pom-poms than you need and have some left over, save them to use for other craft projects.

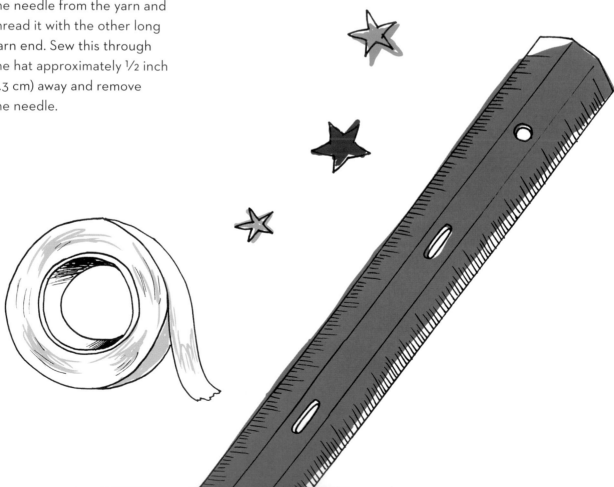

2. Take one of the pom-poms and thread a large, sharp needle with one of the long yarn ends. Start decorating the hat in the center of the front. Sew the yarn through the hat slightly above the rim, so the pom-pom sits just on the edge. Then remove the needle from the yarn and thread it with the other long yarn end. Sew this through the hat approximately ½ inch (1.3 cm) away and remove the needle.

3. Turn the hat inside out and pull both yarn ends through so that the pom-pom is flush against the outside of the hat. Knot the yarn ends together several times to make them secure, taking care not to pull them too tightly and pucker the hat. Then trim away the excess yarn.

4. Repeat steps 2–3, adding another pom-pom a little farther up the hat. Then repeat until a row of pom-poms runs from the front of the hat to the back.

This cute plush owl is easy to sew and fun to customize with a few embroidery stitches.

MATERIALS AND TOOLS

Felt—1 each in tan, blue, cream, and dark brown, 9 x 12 inches (23 x 30.5 cm) each

Embroidery floss—1 skein each in tan DMC 422, brown DMC 898, aqua DMC 598, and white

Tan and blue thread to match felt, or embroidery flosses

Polyester fiberfill stuffing

Straight pins

Scissors

Embroidery needle

Template (see *pg. 136–137*)

INSTRUCTIONS

1. Cut out the templates and pin them onto the felt. Cut out two pieces of the owl body, a front and a back.

2. Position the cream eye piece and blue wing piece on a tan body piece and pin them in place. Stitch them on using the stab stitch. Stitch on the beak piece in the same way.

3. Now add embroidery. The most basic embroidery stitch is the straight stitch. Just tie a knot in the end of your floss, thread it through the needle, and push the needle up through the back of the felt to the front. Push the needle back through a little ways away and pull the floss smoothly against the felt. That's a straight stitch! Use the straight stitch to make the lines on the owl's wing. When you are done stitching lines, tie a knot at the back of the felt and cut off the extra thread.

4. Several straight stitches stitched close together and side by side make a satin stitch. Use the satin stitch to create the open eye. Make a tiny satin stitch in white on the eye for a shine.

5. Two straight stitches that cross each other are called a cross stitch. Make several cross stitches on the owl's body.

6. Finish off the eyes by making several straight stitches coming out from the around the owl's eyes.

7. Make a lazy daisy stitch by making a loop in the floss and catching it with another tiny stitch at the top. Make lazy daisy stitches above the owl's eyes. It's really easy to use these simple stitches to create embroidered embellishments on this owl or on any fabric craft projects.

8. Pin the front and back pieces of the owl together, right sides out. Using tan thread (or two threads from a piece of tan embroidery floss) and the whip stitch, start at the bottom of the owl and begin sewing the front and back pieces together. Keep the stitches small and close together. Switch to blue thread to sew around the blue wing.

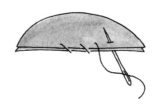

9. When about 2 inches (5 cm) are left to sew the owl shut, stuff the owl with fiberfill until it is nicely plump. Now sew up the hole for a fine, feathered friend.

Jane Bailet Kohlenstein

MOD PODGE FABRIC-SCRAP BOWL

This pretty little bowl is perfect for catching all sorts of treasures!

MATERIALS AND TOOLS

Bowl (about 4 inches (10 cm) top diameter, 2 inches (5 cm) bottom base diameter, and 2½ inches (6.4 cm) height)

Fabric scraps

Plastic wrap

Mod Podge

Foam brush

Scissors

Newspaper

INSTRUCTIONS

1. To begin, cut out the following fabric scraps.

   - Fabric squares: approximately 4 × 4 inches (10 × 10 cm), two for each bowl

   - *Fabric strips: approximately 1–2 inches (2.5-5 cm) wide and 4 inches (10 cm) long, about twelve strips

NOTE:

These sizes and amounts are based on the size of the bowl pictured. A larger bowl will require larger fabric squares or more strips.

2. Prepare the bowl by first covering the outside with plastic wrap. Fold a bit of extra plastic wrap toward the inside of the bowl as well, to protect it from the Mod Podge.

3. Flip the bowl upside down on a protected surface, as Mod Podge is messy and drippy (newspaper works well). Using the foam brush, liberally apply Mod Podge over the outside of the bowl.

4. Begin adding the fabric strips once the bowl is covered with Mod Podge. The first layer of fabric strips will be the *inside* the finished bowl; so, the fabric needs to be placed onto the bowl form with the *front side* facing the bowl.

5. Center a square piece of fabric over the bottom of the bowl (right side facing the bottom, which will be the interior of the finished bowl) and place it down on the

bowl. Using Mod Podge and a foam brush, gently press and smooth the fabric down the sides of the bowl. After the square scrap is in place, begin adding strips of fabric with the right side (the front) facing the bowl, beginning at the top edge of the bowl (this is close to the newspaper) and then adding additional strips to fill in any spaces between the first strips and the fabric square. Use the foam brush to smooth and manipulate the strips into place, just as you did initially with the first square fabric scrap. Make sure the fabric strips are wet with Mod Podge in order for them to stick to each other and the plastic-wrapped bowl.

6. After the first (inside) layer of fabric strips are placed onto the bowl, gently apply another coat of Mod Podge over the fabric strips. Be careful not to move any of the strips or bunch them up.

7. Next, add the strips for the outer layer. This layer will be on the *exterior* of the finished bowl. These strips will need to be placed onto the bowl with right (front) sides facing up. Add fabric the same way you did for the first layer, but this time with the right (front) side facing up. Begin with the square piece, followed by the edges, and then fill in the spaces between.

8. Coat liberally one more time with Mod Podge once the bowl is completely covered with the second layer of fabric. Set aside to dry.

Although drying time will vary, it will most likely take about 24 hours.

9. Gently remove the fabric from the plastic-wrapped bowl once it is dry. Trim and even out any fabric overhang at the edges, and a beautiful fabric bowl is done!

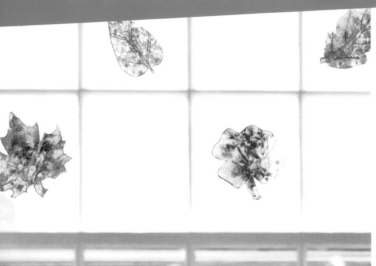

Selina Hoit

CRAYON STAINED GLASS*

CRAFT 3

With colors so vibrant and autumn-like, this is perfect for the fall, but changing the colors is a great way to decorate for any season!

MATERIALS AND TOOLS

Old rag, or paper towels
Wax paper
Pencil sharpener
Old crayons
Iron
Black permanent marker
Scissors
Hole punch (optional)
Template (see pg. 138-139)

*This project requires adult supervision.

INSTRUCTIONS

1. Lay out an old rag or paper towels on a work surface and then place a sheet of wax paper on top.

2. With a pencil sharpener, shave the crayons onto the wax paper. Have fun with your color pattern and arrangement.

3. Spread out the shavings thinly (you do not want large clumps) and lay another piece of wax paper over your crayon-shavings design.

4. Have an adult set an iron to the lowest setting (no steam). Carefully iron directly on the top sheet of wax paper until the crayon shavings are all melted. You will see that you don't need to press very hard and the melting happens quite quickly. Make sure to use a large piece of wax paper with your design in the center; otherwise, some of the crayon shavings may squeeze out and onto your rag and get on the iron. If that happens, quickly rub the iron with an the old rag to get the melted crayon off.

5. Now create a clear workspace and place the leaf template under the wax paper masterpiece. (You can also search the Internet for a your own fun-shaped template). Trace the shape onto the wax paper with a black permanent marker.

6. Carefully cut out the shape without bending the wax and enjoy!

TIP

Using a variety of leaves for your template can make a beautiful decoration for your home or classroom. Some other seasonal ideas: use green crayon shavings with red dots for Christmas trees, or white and blue for a snowman. Hang them in your window and let the fun begin!

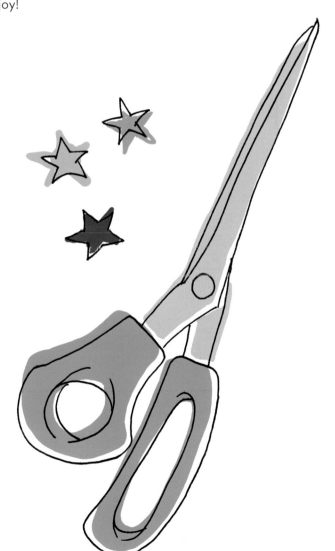

Gwen Diehn

TREASURE BOX HIDDEN IN A BOOK

Need a secret hiding spot? Fill the secret compartment with small treasures, close the book, and put it on a bookshelf with similar books—no one will ever know!

MATERIALS AND TOOLS

1 used hardcover book that no one else wants, at least 1½ inches (3.8 cm) thick

1 empty mint tin

Pencil

Ruler

Scissors

Newspapers or plastic

Plastic grocery bag

Empty yogurt container or other plastic cup

White craft glue

1-inch (2.5 cm) wide inexpensive paintbrush from a hardware store

Water

Sponge or rag

Several heavy books

Mod Podge

INSTRUCTIONS

1. Measure the height (thickness) of the mint tin. Add ½ inch (1.3 cm) to this measurement. The total is the depth the treasure compartment needs to be. Place the book flat on a table and hold the ruler vertically alongside the outside of the pages. Find the number on the ruler that matches the depth you calculated and place a piece of paper between the pages to show where the top of the treasure compartment will be. For example, if the tin is ½-inch (1.3 cm) deep and ½ inch (1.3 cm) was added to that number, the top of the tin will be buried 1 inch (2.5 cm) from the bottom of the book.

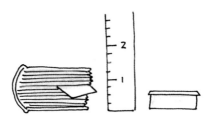

2. Open the book to the marked page and place the tin in the middle of the page. Trace around the tin. Remove the tin and draw lines about ¼ inch (0.6 cm) outside the tin outline on all four sides. Use the ruler to help make the lines straight.

3. Lift the page with the tracing on it and fold it in half toward the spine, creasing it gently. Half the rectangle will be on one side of the center crease and half on the other side. Now cut out the entire rectangle.

4. Smooth this page flat again, and trace around the inside of the cut-out rectangle. Turn the already-cut page to the left, and cut the newly marked page just as the first. Repeat this step for all the remaining pages in the book. This is a big job! Be sure to take a break now and then.

Maybe someone can help with this part of the project.

5. When this is done, there will be a rectangular hole cut through many pages of the book, right down to the back cover. Test the size of the hole by slipping the mint tin inside. The book should close completely, so it's impossible to tell that anything is hidden inside.

6. If the book doesn't close, trace and cut a few more pages from the left side of the book (the pages with the lower numbers) to deepen the hole. If the book closes well, go to the next step.

7. Fill about one-third of the yogurt cup with white craft glue and another third with water. Stir with the brush. The water will thin the glue so it will soak into the pages easily. Prepare the book by slipping the left side of it (the side not cut) into the plastic grocery bag to protect it from the glue.

8. Cover the work surface and brush watery glue onto the edges of all the pages that have rectangles cut out of them. Being a bit sloppy here is fine. The idea is for the watery glue to soak a little way into the pages to glue them all together. Be sure to brush some glue between the bottom pages and inside back cover of the book.

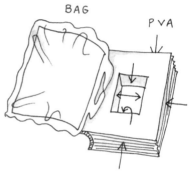

BAG

PVA

9. Pour out the remaining watery glue, and fill about a quarter of the yogurt cup with glue alone. Brush the undiluted glue along all the edges of the cut rectangular space so they stick together. (See illustration for all the places to brush with glue mixed with water and with glue alone.)

10. Remove the plastic bag. Wipe off any glue spills or splashes from the cover, the bag, and the table. Wash out the brush with clean water. Put the dry grocery bag between the secret compartment pages and the uncut pages and close the book. Place several heavy books on top of this book for at least 30 minutes.

11. After 30 minutes, remove the weights from the book and open it. Remove the plastic bag so that the book can air dry completely.

12. While the book is drying, decorate the container cover of the tin with flat objects such as pressed leaves or flowers, pretty paper, artwork, photographs, or magazine pictures. Brush the back of all the items with glue or Mod Podge. Attach them to the cover and press until they are smooth and flat. When

they are all in place, brush glue or Mod Podge over everything to seal the cover and give it a finish coat. Let dry overnight.

13. Fill the secret compartment with small treasures, close the book, and put it on a bookshelf with similar books. No one will know it has a secret treasure box inside it!

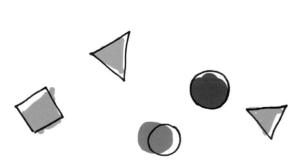

Kajsa Kinsella
SUPER STAR*

CRAFT 3

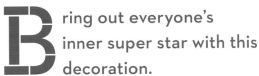

Bring out everyone's inner super star with this decoration.

MATERIALS AND TOOLS

Card stock in turquoise blue, apple green, light pink, sun yellow, and white

Patterned paper in four colors

Glitter paper in green, yellow, blue, and pink

Scissors

Patterned craft scissors

Ink pads

Flower rubber stamps

Flat-backed gems

White craft glue or glue stick

Tweezers

Thin paintbrush

Ribbon

Hole punch

Paper guillotine (optional)

*This project requires adult supervision.

INSTRUCTIONS

1. Cut eight 8¼ x 4 inches (21 x 10 cm) rectangles of patterned paper, two of each pattern. Fold each in half neatly and crease the fold firmly.

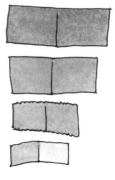

TIP

Many rectangles are used in this project, so keep them separated and in neat piles to make it easier to find them at each step. Cut them out with a scissors or ask an adult to help cut them on a paper guillotine.

2. Cut eight rectangles 7⅛ x 3⅜ inches (18 x 8.6 cm) of glittery paper. Crease and fold them.

3. Using craft scissors, cut eight pieces of colored card stock 5½ x 2⅞ inches (14 x 7.5 cm). Crease and fold them.

4. Using regular scissors, cut eight rectangles of white card stock to 4 x 1¾ inches (10 x 4.5 cm). Crease and fold them.

5. Unfold one piece of each of the three largest sizes and glue together *only* the top parts, as shown. Make eight star pieces. Set aside to dry.

6. Choose pretty flower rubber stamps and go to town decorating the white rectangles. Use ink colors that match the colored paper strips. Glue on some sparkly gems to add a bit of extra bling! Dab on a tiny bit of glue and use tweezers to place them on the card stock.

7. To assemble the star, first check that all sides are straight and neat. When they are, glue the eight star parts together back to back, as shown, but do not glue the first and the last

side together. Leave them to dry thoroughly.

8. Glue the decorated white inner pieces to the center of each of the star parts. Remember to glue only at the top strip, as was done in step 5, or the star won't open later.

9. Holding the first and the last sides together, look at the star. Isn't it amazing! Punch a single hole through both the first and last sides, one side at a time.

10. Cut a piece of a cheerful ribbon, fold it in half, and push it through both holes. Make a loop, tie the ends together in a square knot, and hang the star in the sun to catch the sparkle.

Ashley Little

ARM-KNITTED SCARF*

CRAFT
4

Experienced knitters will pick up arm knitting in no time! Beginners: consider this an introductory knitting tutorial. To make an arm-knitted scarf for an adult, just buy an extra skein of yarn.

MATERIALS AND TOOLS

1 skein Lion Brand Wool Ease Thick & Quick yarn in Cobalt #640-107, or any other super bulky weight yarn

Scissors

*This project requires adult supervision.

INSTRUCTIONS

Casting On

1. Hold two strands of yarn together. To do this using only one skein of yarn, pull one end of yarn from the inside of the skein and pull the other end of yarn from the outside of the skein. These two pieces will be held and used together throughout the project.

2. Make a slipknot with the yarn by forming a circle about 3 inches (7.5 cm) across on a flat surface. Leave a 56 inch (142 cm) long yarn tail.

3. Hold onto the circle where it crosses over itself with one hand and pull the tail under the middle of the circle with the other. Pull the center piece up through the circle to make a loop. Do not tighten it at this time.

4. Slip that loop onto your right arm and pull it so that the loop is smaller but still loose enough to slip over your hand.

5. Cast on the rest of the base stitches from the long tail. With your left hand, grasp the two pieces of yarn that are attached to the skein. Wrap the yarn behind your left thumb while using your ring and pinkie fingers of the same hand to press it against your palm and hold it tightly.

6. Hold the long tail end of the yarn between your pointer and middle fingers.

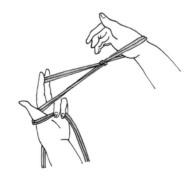

7. Slide your right hand up between the loop of yarn wrapped around your left thumb.

8. With your right hand inside the yarn loop, grasp the yarn tail that you are holding between your left pointer and middle fingers.

9. Pull the tail through the loop around your left thumb to form a second loop. Leave the new loop open and loose.

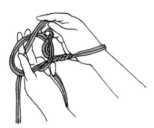

10. Place that loop on your right hand beside your slipknot loop and tighten it just enough to match the size of the slipknot loop. You now have two cast-on stitches. (While you are doing this step, don't let go of the pieces of yarn in your left hand. You will need them to make the rest of the slipknots.)

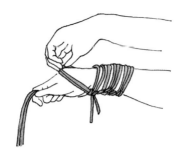

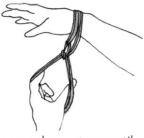

11. Repeat these steps until you have seven loops on your right arm. (Remember that the slipknot counts as a loop too!)

Knitting the First Row

1. Now you are going to knit the first row, which means that all the loops on your right arm will move over to your left arm as you knit.

2. With your right hand, grasp the yarn that is attached to the skein. (Yes, all the loops are still on your right arm when you do this.) Hang onto the skein yarn as you pull the first loop off your right arm with your left hand. You are pulling the loop over the skein yarn, so don't let go of the yarn in your right fingers!

3. Pull the skein yarn though the loop you have just pulled off your right arm and hand to make a new loop. Place that new loop over on your left arm.

4. Pull the yarn firmly, just like you did the slipknot, making sure the loop is just big enough to slide over your left hand. Now you have one loop on your left arm and six still on your right arm.

5. Repeat these steps until all the loops from your right arm are now on your left arm.

Knitting the Second Row

1. Now let's knit all those loops on your left arm back over to your right arm. Grab the yarn with your left hand. With your right hand, pull the first loop from your left arm off your hand and repeat the steps used to knit the first row but moving from your left hand to your right.

2. Place the new loop onto your right arm.

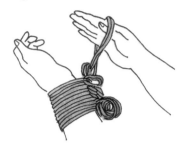

3. Repeat those steps: Grasp the yarn with your left hand and use your right hand to pull the loop from your left arm right over your left hand.

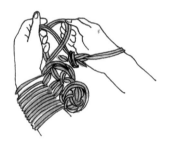

4. Place the loop on your right arm.

5. Once all the loops are on your right arm again, continue to arm-knit, switching arms for each new row, until your scarf measures the length you'd like.

Binding Off

1. Once the scarf has reached the right length, you'll need to get those loops off your arm. To do that, first knit two stitches, just as you did for each row of the scarf. You have two loops on your left arm and five on your right arm.

2. Now pull the first knitted stitch loop on your left arm back over the second knitted stitch loop.

3. Drop that loop, so you have only one loop on your left arm. Don't worry, the dropped loop won't unravel!

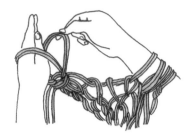

4. Knit another stitch, then repeat steps 2–3, pulling the loops over each other to bind off.

5. When you only have one stitch left on your arm, pull the loop off your arm. Cut the yarn, leaving about a 3-inch (7.5 cm) tail. Insert the tail into the loop you just removed from your arm and pull the yarn end through to secure it.

Weaving in the Ends

1. You've probably noticed that you have one end of yarn hanging out on each end of your scarf. Cut the long end to about 3 inches (7.5 cm) to match the shorter end.

2. To get rid of both ends, just weave them back and forth through your stitches to hide them.

Suzie Millions

BALLOONY BIRDS*

H ere's a unique project that will quickly replace traditional balloon animals at your next gathering.

MATERIALS AND TOOLS

- 4 lbs. (1.8 kg) plaster of paris
- Water, 24 ounces (0.7 L) plus a little extra water (room temperature) for mix and more to fill a tub
- 24-ounce (0.7 L) plastic water bottle with sports cap
- Scissors
- Several small balloons (Do not use water balloons, as they are too thin and will not work.)
- Small bucket (2½-quart (2.37 L) paint pail works well)
- Paint clothes
- Rubber gloves
- Plastic funnel
- 2 disposable plastic 8-ounce (0.24 L) cups
- Paint stirrer
- Rags
- Large bucket or tub
- Plastic crate or sturdy box, at least 12 inches (30 cm) tall (the filled balloons need to hang while drying.)
- 2 pieces of string, 6 inches (15.2 cm) each
- Fine, waterproof sandpaper
- 2 pieces of colorful plastic drinking straw cut into 3-inch (7.2 cm) lengths
- 6 glass-headed pins
- 4 upholstery tacks, black or brown
- Acrylic craft paint in 2 bright colors plus blacklight pink
- Bright feathers
- Plastic fork
- 1-inch (2.5 cm) wide paintbrush
- Quick-setting craft glue

*This project requires adult supervision.

TIP

This is a messy craft project, so put on painting clothes and set up the following outdoor work areas:

- *MIXING AREA (the messiest spot): Small bucket, water bottle, plaster, one 8-ounce (0.24 L) cup, paint stirrer, funnel*
- *RINSING AREA (the wet spot): Large bucket or tub filled with water, rags*
- *DRYING AREA (the try-to-keep-it-clean spot): Crate or box, string, scissors, cup with the pieces of drinking straw, pins, tacks*

NOTES

1. Plaster and plumbing do not mix. Never rinse anything with plaster on it in a sink; never pour leftover plaster down plumbing. 2. Plaster gets hot as it dries and should never be left on your skin. If you get any on yourself, immediately rinse it off (see the Tip box about setting up a rinsing area).

INSTRUCTIONS

1. Remove the screen from the nozzle of the plastic water bottle by carefully cutting the tip out with scissors. You may need an adult to help with this.

2. In the mixing area, put on a pair of gloves. Add 24 ounces (0.7 L) (three 8-ounce (0.2 L) cups) of room-temperature water to the small bucket. One at a time, shake six 8-ounce (0.24 L) cups of plaster into the bucket of water, scattering it evenly over the top. Do not stir yet; let the plaster sink in by itself. After it sits for 2 minutes, blend the plaster and water with the stirrer to make it smooth; it should be thicker than chocolate syrup but thinner than a milkshake.

3. Put the funnel in the water bottle and slowly pour the mix into it until there is enough mix in the funnel to fill the bottle. (Adult help may be needed for the lifting and pouring.) Clean the empty funnel in the large rinse bucket and wipe your gloved hands on a rag.

4. Blow up a balloon about the size of a large orange. Twist the balloon neck a couple of times and stretch the end of it over the nozzle of the bottle.

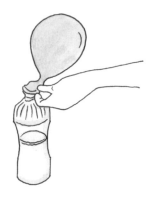

5. Still keeping the balloon neck twisted, hold the balloon on the bottle with one hand, hold the bottle with the other hand and turn it upside down so the balloon is resting on the work surface and the bottle is up above it. Let the neck of the balloon untwist so it can fill. Keep holding the balloon on the bottle while the mix runs into it. Squeeze the bottle a little, but not too hard. Use just over half the contents of the bottle to make the large bird first. When the bottle is a little more than half empty, twist the balloon neck a couple of times to seal it and take it off of the bottle, still holding it closed. Set the bottle aside for now.

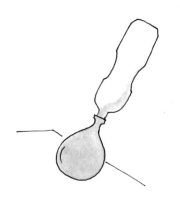

6. This step is messy. Point the end of the balloon away from you, let the neck untwist, and let out a little bit of air. First, plaster will spit from the balloon and then it will begin to pour. When it begins to pour, twist the neck again a few times and then tie it in a knot. Dip the balloon in the big rinse bucket to wash off any plaster on the outside. To hang the balloon while it dries, tie a piece of string tightly on the balloon neck, slip the other end through the top of the crate or box, and tie it again. Fill the balloon for the smaller bird with the rest of the mix in the bottle and hang that balloon too.

7. Ask an adult to carefully poke two sets of two holes in the top of the box to thread the string through so the balloons can hang to dry, Keep them far enough apart so the filled balloons do not touch while drying. The balloons will get hot as the plaster dries. Let them dry enough to be handled without losing their shape, about 10–30 minutes, depending on the size of the balloons and the weather. They are ready when they feel more like a tomato than a water balloon (not dry enough) or an apple (too dry). The small one will dry faster than the big one. When the smaller one is ready, cut it down and take it and the scissors to the mixing area. Point the knotted end of the balloon away (there might be a little water collected in the neck), stretch out the knot from the balloon, and use the scissors to cut it off as close to the plaster as possible. Pull the rest of the balloon away from the plaster, rolling it down and away. Try not to scrape or scratch the plaster, but it should be soft enough to smooth over any accidental marks. It will dry very quickly now.

8. Push the piece of drinking straw into the plaster for a beak; then push in the upholstery tacks to make the eyes, and the glass-headed pins on top of the bird's head (see illustration). To finish the beak, use the scissors to trim the straw to the desired length and then make a small snip across the straw to split it. Pull the top and bottom away from each other a little to open the beak. Using the plastic fork, scratch some lines into the bird's chest. Rub away any crumbs of plaster and smooth any rough spots with your thumb.

9. Cut down the large balloon next and finish it the same way as the smaller bird (steps 7 and 8). Let the birds dry overnight before painting and finishing.

Next Day

10. Rub the bottom of either bird over the sandpaper if it needs to be flatter on the bottom so it won't roll over. Sand away any rough spots on the body. Brush away any plaster dust.

11. Paint the chest of each bird bright pink, then use a different color for the rest of the bird. After the paint dries, glue one feather to each side to make the wings and three to the back of each bird to make the tail.

Laura Howard
SPACE MOBILE*

Use colorful craft felt to make a space mobile, complete with a rocket for exploring far-off planets! For safety, make sure the finished mobile hangs well out of the reach of babies and young children.

MATERIALS AND TOOLS

- 1 royal blue felt, 3 x 6 inches (8 x 15 cm)
- 1 light blue felt, 4 x 6 inches (10 x 15 cm)
- 1 turquoise felt, 5 x 7 inches (13 x 18 cm)
- 1 bright green felt, $4\frac{1}{2}$ x $4\frac{1}{2}$ inches (11.5 x 11.5 cm)
- 1 lilac felt, 6 x $6\frac{1}{2}$ inches (15 x 16.5 cm)
- 1 purple felt, $3\frac{1}{2}$ x $3\frac{1}{2}$ inches (9 x 9 cm)
- 1 pink felt, $3\frac{1}{2}$ x $4\frac{1}{2}$ inches (9 x 11 cm)
- 1 white felt, 3 x $4\frac{1}{2}$ inches (8 x 11.5 cm)
- 1 yellow felt, 9 x 12 inches (23 x 30.5 cm)
- 1 orange felt, 6 x 7 inches (15 x 18 cm)
- 1 red felt, 5 x 7 inches (13 x 18 cm)
- 1 narrow orange ribbon, 19 inches (48 cm)

- Sewing threads to match the felt colors
- "Invisible" plastic sewing thread
- 1 mobile ring or the inner ring of an embroidery hoop, 6–7 inches (15 x 18 cm) in diameter (The hoop used in this project is a plastic ring designed for use with Hama beads.)
- Templates (see pg. 140–141)
- Scissors
- Sewing needle
- Straight pins
- Sewing scissors

*This project requires adult supervision.

INSTRUCTIONS

THE MOON, STARS, AND SMALL PLANET PIECES

1. Use the templates to cut 2 white moons; 8 yellow small stars; 6 yellow large stars; and 2 lilac, 2 pink, 2 turquoise, and 2 red small circles.

2. Hold or pin two matching pieces together and sew around the edges of the moon, stars, and small planets with running stitches, using a matching-color sewing thread. Running stitches look like this - - - - - .

THE GAS GIANT

1. Use the templates to cut two large circles from lilac felt and one of each of the six gas giant pieces from purple felt.

2. Arrange the small pieces on one of the circles, as pictured, and sew them in place. Use running stitches and matching sewing thread. Don't sew around the outside edge of the circle; that will be sewn very soon.

3. Hold or pin the decorated circle to the undecorated one and sew them together with a line of running stitches in matching (lilac) thread.

THE EARTH

1. Use the templates provided to cut two medium circles, from royal blue felt and one of each of the four land pieces from bright green felt.

2. Follow the steps for the gas giant.

RINGED PLANETS

1. Use the templates to cut 2 orange and 2 light blue medium circles and 2 bright green and 2 pink rings.

2. Hold or pin two matching circles together. Join them together by sewing a line of running stitches around the edge using matching sewing thread.

3. Position the contrasting ring pieces just above the center of the circle (making a "sandwich" with the circle in between the two ring pieces) and hold or pin them in place. Sew the ring pieces together with running stitches and matching sewing thread, sewing through all four layers

where needed and turning the planet over several times while sewing to keep the stitches neat and in line.

VARIATION

To add sequins to the ringed planet, it might be helpful to pin the ring in position before starting so the sequins are sewn in the right place. Sew each sequin in position with three stitches of matching sewing thread, or use fabric glue and add them to the pieces when all other sewing is finished. Let the glue dry completely before constructing the mobile.

SUN

1. Use the templates to cut 2 yellow large circles and 1 orange sunburst.

2. Hold or pin the pieces together, making a "sandwich" with the sunburst in the middle of the two circles.

3. Sew a line of running stitches around the circle with matching sewing thread, sewing all three layers together. Turn the sun over several times while sewing to keep the stitches neat and in line.

ROCKET

1. Use the templates provided to cut 1 rocket top and 2 rocket fins from red felt, 1 rocket window from light blue felt, and 2 rockets from turquoise felt.

2. Pin the rocket top and window to one of the rocket pieces and sew them in place with running stitches and matching sewing thread. Sew only along the bottom edge of the rocket top as the other edges will be sewn later.

3. Cut 4 pieces of narrow orange ribbon (4¾ inches; 12 cm each), cutting the ends at an angle to help prevent fraying. Sew the ribbons to the bottom of one of the rocket fin pieces, as pictured. Use a whipstitch and matching red sewing thread and try to sew into the felt but not through it.

4. Hold or pin the 2 fin pieces together so the sewn-on ribbon ends are hidden between them. Sew the felt layers together with running stitch and matching thread.

5. Place the red fin piece between the 2 turquoise rocket pieces so the curved fins stick out on each side and the nozzles (with their ribbon flames) stick out at the bottom. Pin or hold the layers together and sew them together with a line of running stitches around the rocket, using matching turquoise sewing thread.

TO CONSTRUCT THE MOBILE

1. Arrange the finished moon, sun, stars, planets, and rocket in four vertical rows. These will be the four strands of the mobile.

2. Cut 4 long pieces of "invisible" plastic sewing thread. These pieces need to be long enough for hanging a strand from the mobile's

hoop and also for hanging the mobile, so think about where it will be displayed! Tie a large knot in the end of the thread and then use long running stitches to sew the felt pieces onto the thread, working from the bottom piece upward. Sew from the back of each piece and try to sew into the felt but not through it. Repeat this step for each strand of the mobile.

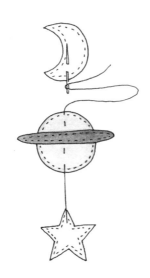

3. Tie each strand to one "corner" of the mobile hoop and knot them in place. Next, join all 4 threads in the center (making sure the hoop hangs level) and knot them together. Then, either leave the threads loose until hanging the mobile or tie them securely in a loop for hanging, cutting away any excess thread.

Suzie Millions

SAND CANDLES*

CRAFT

4

L ooking for something different as a gift? These illuminating creations will surely impress.

MATERIALS AND TOOLS

- Damp, but not soggy, sand
- ½ pound (225 g) household paraffin wax
- Several 2-inch (5 cm) wire wicks with base tabs
- 4 or more crayons in various colors, paper peeled off
- Small plastic dish tub or bucket
- Ruler
- Old electric coffeemaker and coffeepot
- Popsicle sticks (or small straight twigs from trees)
- Paint stirrer
- 1-inch (2.5 cm) paintbrush
- Sharp knife (can be a craft or kitchen knife)

*This project requires adult supervision.

NOTES

- *You need to exercise caution when melting and handling hot wax. Ask an adult for help. An old coffeemaker from a thrift store is ideal for this project, because it melts the wax and keeps it a safe, even temperature. Plus, the handle and pour spout make pouring hot wax a lot safer than using a pan or a tin can set in hot water. But do heed these cautions:*

- *Wax can ignite at high temperatures; that's why using a coffeemaker is a good idea. If you're not using one, please follow the instructions on the package of paraffin, which most likely suggests melting the wax in a double boiler.*

- *If you're using a coffeemaker, unplug it immediately after pouring the last candle. Never leave heated wax unattended.*

- *Clean the coffeepot by pouring out all the unused wax and running hot water through it. Hot water lifts off wax stuck to the sides of the pot. Pour out the water outside, not down the drain, because it can damage indoor plumbing. Don't use the coffeepot you make coffee in; some wax residue will remain.*

INSTRUCTIONS

1. Put ½ a pound (225 g) of wax in the bottom of the coffeepot. Break a crayon into several pieces and add half of them to the wax. Turn the coffeemaker on without water in it. The warming plate under the coffeepot will melt the wax completely in about 30 minutes.

TIP

These candles can be made directly in sand at the seashore. Otherwise, add 2 inches (5 cm) of sand to a small plastic dish tub or bucket. Mix in enough water to make a handful of damp sand hold its shape when squeezed.

2. Push your fist down into the sand to make a hole. The shape will resemble a clamshell. Make a hole for each candle you plan to make.

3. Make the legs for each candle by pushing your pinky finger down into each candle hole 3 times. Try to make the leg holes the same depth so the candles will stand evenly and not dip too much to one side.

4. Put a wick up in the middle of each candle hole.

5. Put 2 popsicle sticks across each hole, sandwiching the wick between them to keep it standing up straight.

6. Carefully stir the wax and crayon with the paint stirrer. Adjust the color by adding more crayon pieces. Continue to stir the wax until the wax and crayons are completely melted.

7. For each candle, very slowly pour the wax into the legs first and then into the rest of the candle. Don't pour the wax directly over the wick. It's OK if wax spills over the hole a little and spreads out.

8. When you are finished filling all the candle holes, put the coffeepot back on the coffeemaker hot plate and turn off the unit.

9. The candles are set when the entire top surface is firm, about 30 minutes, depending on how big they are. Be careful not to remove them from the sand too soon or the top of the candle will sink down over the legs.

10. Use a paintbrush to remove any extra sand from the wax.

11. Candles must be level. If they aren't, burning wax will run downhill and extinguish the flame. If any of the candles aren't level, ask an adult to trim the legs with a sharp knife to even them out.

Gwen Diehn

SNACK-BAG NOTEBOOK*

Never feel guilty about finishing a bag of chips again with this crafty way of recycling used snack bags!

MATERIALS AND TOOLS

- 1 empty snack food bag, with the top cut off in a straight line as close to the top as possible
- 1 roll of clear packaging tape, about 1½ inches (3.8 cm) wide
- 1 roll of duct tape, any color
- 25 pieces of 8½ x11 inch (or A4—21 x 29.7 cm) blank paper, such as computer paper
- 2 yards of heavy thread, such as fishing twine, bookbinder's thread, buttonhole thread, or waxed dental floss
- Needle with a big enough eye for the thread you have chosen
- Scissors
- Large paper clip or bone folder for smoothing creases
- 10 small binder clips (Ask for ¾-inch (2 cm) binder clips at an office supply store)
- Pushpin or an awl for punching holes in paper
- Needle-nose pliers
- Pencil
- Scrap paper the height of the short side of the pages and 2 inches (5 cm) wide
- Old telephone book or thick magazine

*This project requires adult supervision.

INSTRUCTIONS

1. Wash out the bag carefully with a little dish detergent and water. Use a towel to dry out the inside and outside completely. After the bag is thoroughly dry, flatten it.

2. Place the bag on the table horizontally (with the wide side going across) and fold it in half (like a book) to find the center. Firmly crease the centerfold to mark it. Open the bag and turn it with the side chosen to be the outside facing up. Place a strip of clear tape down the centerfold from top to bottom to reinforce the bag on the spine where there will be holes for stitches. Carefully trim off any extra tape.

3. Turn the bag over so the inside is facing up. Fold the bag the same way as in step 2, and again crease the centerfold to mark it. Open the bag again and cover the centerfold from top to bottom with a strip of duct tape. Trim any extra duct tape.

4. With the inside of the bag still facing up, place strips of duct tape close to all four edges. These strips of tape will reinforce the hem

(running) stitches on all sides of the book. Now fold a double hem, with each fold ¼-inch (6 mm) deep on all four sides, clipping the hem in place with binder clips. These hems must be sewn. Use a paper clip or bone folder to firmly crease the hem folds before going on to step 5.

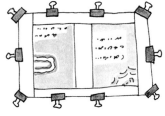

5. Thread the needle with 1 yard (1 m) of thread and make a knot in the bottom of one end of it. Sew ¼-inch (6 mm) running stitches, beginning at a corner. Before putting the needle into the thick corner hem, place the bag over the old telephone book and poke a hole in the corner with the awl or pushpin. (Ask an adult for help, if needed.) If the needle still gets stuck, use the needle-nose pliers to pull it through the hole. Sew the hem on all sides of the bag, going back to the first corner. Push the needle into the first

corner hole. Pull the needle through the corner hole. Lap the edge and tie a knot by slipping the needle under the last stitch and then back through the loop. Pull the thread firmly to make a knot.

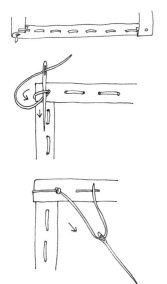

6. Place the cover, inside facing up, on the table. Measure the distance between the top of the bottom hem and the bottom of the top hem and write down that number. This will be the height of the pages. Now measure the distance between the inside edges of the side hems. Write down that number and subtract 1 from it. This is the width of the folded-out pages. Ask an adult to help cut the 25 pieces of paper into rectangles as high and as wide as the written measurements. For example,

the pages in the sample book are 5 x 9 inches (6 x 22 cm) before folding, because the measurements between the hems were 5 x 10 inches (5.7 x 25.4 cm).

7. Fold all 25 pages in half, side to side. Fold them one at a time. Use the paper clip to smooth the creases and make the folded pages as flat as possible. After folding all the pages, make five booklets of five pages each.

8. With a pushpin or awl, punch holes in each booklet and in the cover to prepare for sewing the pages into the cover. Make a pattern using the piece of scrap paper that is the exact height of the paper booklets and about 2 inches (5 cm) wide. Fold the strip of paper in half the long way. Then fold it in half the short way and make a pencil mark where the two folds cross. Mark the crease with a pencil halfway between the center mark and the top of the scrap paper and halfway to the bottom. This pattern of three dots will help in marking in the same place in each booklet crease. Write a T for top at the top of the pattern.

9. Place the closed telephone book or magazine on top of the old phone book. Place the cover on top, with the inside facing you. Open the first booklet and place it on top of the inside cover with the centerfold creases aligned. Use four binder clips to clip the booklet to the cover. Place the pattern on the crease of the booklet. Use a pushpin or awl to make three holes through all five sheets of the booklet and the cover. When all three holes are punched, remove the pattern and resecure the clips.

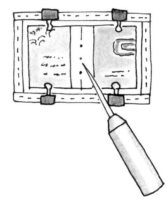

10. To sew, put the needle (no need to knot the thread) into the center hole starting from the outside of the cover toward the inside, leaving a 3–4-inch (7–10 cm) tail hanging on the outside of the cover. Clip the tail in place with a binder clip. Gently pull the thread through the center hole. Then from

the inside, push the needle into the top hole and pull it through to the outside of the cover. Now bring the needle to the bottom hole, skipping over the center hole with the tail. Pull the thread from the inside until the long stitch across the center hole on the outside is flat and tight. Push the needle back into the center hole from the inside. The needle will come out on the outside where a long stitch is. Be sure the needle comes out on the opposite side of the long stitch from the tail. (See figure 6.) Cut the thread off, leaving another tail of about 3–4 inches (7–10 cm) long. Tie the two tails together over the long stitch. Trim the ends to about ½-inch (1.3 cm) long.

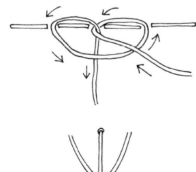

11. To punch and sew the rest of the booklets, first open the cover and close the first booklet. Line up the next booklet with the edge of the already-sewn booklet. (To keep the first booklet in the center, sew two booklets into the cover one at a time. Sew one on the left side, and then one on the right side until all four are sewn in.) Be careful to leave a small gap between the folded edges of the booklets so that the holes in the cover will be at least ⅛ inch (0.3 cm) from each other. Repeat steps 9 and 10. Until all five are securely sewn and tied into the cover for a one-of-a-kind notebook!

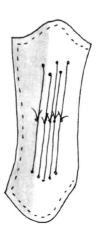

Anne B. Weil
POM-POMS IN BULK*

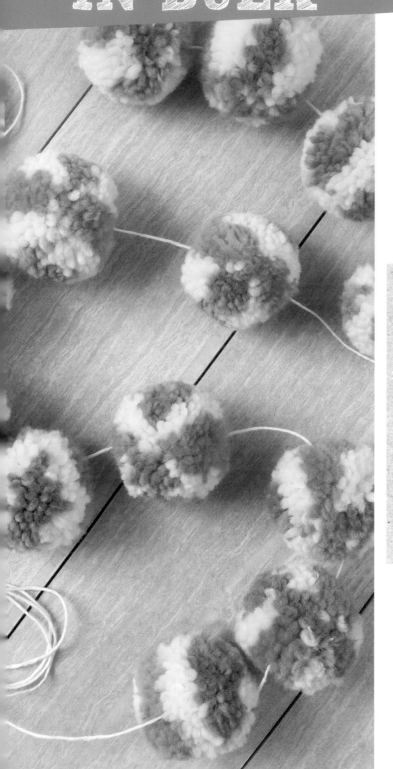

Three cheers to decorating almost anything with a lot of colorful pom-poms after mastering this technique!

MATERIALS AND TOOLS

Table, bench, or chair with legs that can be turned upside down on top of another table.

One skein Lion Brand Yarn Alpine Wool, 100% wool, bay leaf (123)

One skein Lion Brand Yarn Alpine Wool, 100% wool, vanilla (099)

One skein Paton's Classic Wool Roving Yarn, 100% wool, yellow

Approximately 4 yards (3.7 m) of twine or embroidery thread

Scissors

*This project requires adult supervision.

INSTRUCTIONS

1. Turn table or chair upside down on top of another table so the legs point upward and are approximately arm height.

2. Decide on the yarn order. Tie the first skein of yarn to one of the upturned furniture legs.

3. Start wrapping the yarn around the leg opposite, the one farthest away from the starting leg. Wrap the first color approximately 35 times around these two legs.

4. Change colors by tying two colors together with a sliding knot.

5. Trim the ends and continue wrapping the new color approximately 45 times around.

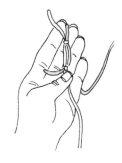

6. Repeat step 4 for the new color. Wrap this color approximately 30 times.

7. Tie off the yarn to one of the legs.

8. With twine or embroidery thread, tie loops around the band of yarn at 2½-inch (6.4 cm) intervals with a surgeon's knot. Make a square knot, wrap the twine around the band a second time in the same place, and make another square knot. Make these ties as tight as possible (each tie will be the center of one pom-pom, so the tighter the better). For the best results, start in the middle between two legs and move from the center toward the legs on each side.

TIP

For bigger pom-poms, tie the band of yarn at 2¾–3-inch (7–7.5 cm) intervals.

9. Cut through the yarn between each of the ties with scissors.

10. Cut halfway through the yarn at a time to make cutting easier.

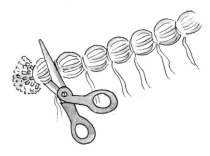

11. Fluff each pom-pom. They will look oblong. Trim them along the edges until they form a circle shape and look even.

12. String twine or embroidery thread through the center circle of each pom-pom and hang them! Super fun and great for a party!!

BATH FIZZIES*

The aroma of the fizzies is fresh and lovely, which makes bath time even more enjoyable!!

MATERIALS AND TOOLS

8 ounces (227 g) baking soda
4 ounces (113.5 g) cornstarch
4 ounces (113.5 g) citric acid
4 ounces (113.5 g) mineral salts
¾ tablespoon (11.25 mL) water
2 teaspoons (10 mL) essential oil (make sure it's safe to use on the body)
2½ tablespoons (37.5 ml) vegetable oil
5 to 6 drops food coloring
Large bowl
Small bowl or a clean jar with a lid
Mixing spoon
Whisk
Flexible silicon molds
Protective eye goggles
Newspapers or plastic

*This project requires adult supervision.

INSTRUCTIONS

TIP

Making bath fizzies can be a very messy job, but there is nothing cooler than bubbling-up the bath with these!

1. Cover a work surface with newspaper or plastic. With an adult's help, mix the dry ingredients (baking soda, cornstarch, citric acid, and mineral salt) together in a large bowl using a mixing spoon. It will be a little dusty, so mix it slowly!

TIP

Always wear protective goggles when handling citric acid, as it can sting the eyes. Wash hands thoroughly after use.

2. Now mix the wet ingredients together in a small bowl or jar (water, essential oil, and food coloring). Don't worry if it does not blend; it will later, when added to the ingredients in the large bowl.

3. Very slowly pour the wet ingredients into the dry ingredients while whisking constantly. Make sure to whisk in every drop very well. The dry ingredients will color and should become moist, like slightly wet sand.

4. When all the ingredients are mixed well, pinch a handful from the bowl and squeeze it to see if it clumps together. If it doesn't, add just a little bit of water and mix well. Pinch another handful and repeat the test. Keep adding water, a little at a time, until the mix clumps when squeezed.

5. Pack flexible silicon molds, such as ice cube trays or candy molds, with the moist mixture. Pack the mixture in really well, or the forms will fall apart when they are dry. Be sure to work on a covered surface because this part is extra messy.

6. Allow them to dry for a few days and then carefully pop them out of the molds. When you use them in the bath, the fizzies will bubble and make a funny popping sound. Hold a fizzie in your hand and then dip it into the water; you will immediately see the fizzing effect. Since they contain oil, two fizzies per bath should do it; otherwise, the water will become too greasy and you might slip.

WATERMELON CROSS STITCH*

CRAFT
4

This tasty design is perfect for mastering the classic stitch.

MATERIALS AND TOOLS

Embroidery needle
Embroidery thread—1 each in red,
    yellow, green, and black
Card stock
Template (see pg. 142)
Small-hole punch
Paperclips or small binder clips

*This project requires adult supervision.

INSTRUCTIONS

1. Clip the template over the card stock and punch the hole pattern into the card stock.

2. Thread the embroidery needle with the black thread and knot the end of the thread.

3. Find the location for the first black cross-stitch. Push the needle from the back of the card stock to the front of hole 1.

4. Pull the thread completely through and push the needle into hole 2. Pull the thread firmly through to form the first side of the cross-stitch.

5. Push the needle from the back to front of hole 3. Keep the stitches firm but not tight enough to bend the card stock.

6. Push the needle through hole 4, front to back, to form the other side of the cross with the thread.

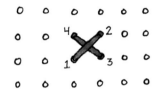

7. Complete all the black crosses and knot the thread in the back of the card stock before changing colors.

8. To embroider a cross-stitch line, thread the needle with red thread and knot the end.

9. Start at the back of the card stock and stitch only one side of a cross in a row from the bottom left to the top right. Complete the entire row.

10. Once the row is complete, stitch from right to left to complete the crosses.

11. Repeat steps 7 and 8 until all the red crosses are done, and then knot off the red thread. Use the bottom of the first row of stitches for the top of the next row. Stitch around the black crosses already made.

10. Repeat the stitches for yellow and green threads.

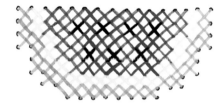

Cynthia Shaffer

STACKABLE SHRINK-PLASTIC RINGS*

CRAFT
4

Whether used as a party favor or as an accessory, these rings stack a lot of fun into one project

MATERIALS AND TOOLS

1 sheet of frosted shrink plastic
Template (see *pg. 133*)
Black erasable marker
Black permanent marker
Scissors
Self-healing craft mat
Craft knife
Soft, disposable cloth
Colored pencils
Oven and cookie sheet
Hot pads
Oven

*This project requires adult supervision.

INSTRUCTIONS

1. Place the shrink plastic onto template A with the frosted (rough) side down.

2. Using the erasable marker, trace template A on the shrink plastic.

3. Use the permanent marker to trace template B (the cupcake) or C–K on the outer part of the traced ring, overlapping onto the ring by ⅛ inch (0.3 cm).

4. Using the scissors, cut out around the outer traced lines.

5. Use a craft knife and self-healing mat to cut out the inside area of the ring. Ask an adult to help with this step.

6. Wipe off the erasable marker from drawing template A.

7. Flip the shrink rings over so that the frosted side is up. Color in the cupcake or other shapes.

8. Place the shrink plastic on a cookie sheet. With an adult's help, bake according to the manufacturer's instructions. Allow to cool completely before touching.

TIP

Make multiple rings with cupcakes, hearts, owls, mushrooms, or flowers and stack them and arrange different combinations for wearing.

CONTRIBUTOR BIOS

TRICE BOERENS

Trice Boerens has worked as an art director, creative editor, product development associate, and photo stylist. She has also authored more than 100 how-to books that cover subjects from paper crafting to furniture refinishing.

ESTHER COOMBS

Esther Coombs is a practicing artist living and working in Hampshire, UK, who believes life is a story and that the narrative is best told with drawings. She creates up-cycled vintage ceramics and products in a shed behind her garden, and they have her hand-drawn illustrations directly on the surface.

Nowadays Esther mostly works on illustrations by commission, as well as small personal pieces, with the aid of her cats, Ivor and Percy, occasional interruption from her young daughter, and the beautiful rural surroundings where she is lucky enough to live. Examples of her work can be seen on her website at www.esthercoombs.com, and her items can be purchased on Etsy at www.esthercoombs.etsy.com.

GWEN DIEHN

Gwen Diehn studied art at Indiana University at South Bend (BA), The University of Notre Dame (MA), and Vermont College (MFA). Her prints, drawings, and artists' books have been exhibited internationally and are in many collections, including the National Museum of Women in the Arts, Washington, DC. She has taught art at the college level and in short courses and workshops for many years. She is the author of several Sterling/Lark books, including *Simple Printmaking* (2000), *Real Life Journals* (*Journal Your Way* paperback title) (2010), and *The Complete Decorated Journal* (2013). She was assisted in developing the projects that are in this book by her ten-year-old granddaughter, Maya Diehn.

AMBER DOHRENWEND

Always looking for the hidden potential in everyday objects, Amber Dohrenwend can often be caught rummaging through a good recyclables pile with her two young daughters and trusty bike by her side. Besides pursuing creative endeavors, such as making anything and everything out of cardboard, Amber has taught around the world at international schools in Taiwan, Egypt, and Pakistan. Tokyo, Japan, is her current home. Read more about Amber's modern cardboard designs, costumes, and pop-up play days at www.thecardboardcollective.com

SELINA HOIT

Selina owns Creative Juices Décor at www.creativejuicesdecor.com. The blog will be sure to get all your Creative Juices flowing! She is an interior designer by degree, artist by heart, and classical musician by years of practice. Selina has a passion for home design/decorating, thrift-store shopping, healthy recipes, and crafting. She also has three young children, so crafts are plentiful on her blog. Come, stop by, be inspired, and walk away with a bunch of fun ideas for your home and family.

LAURA HOWARD

Laura is a designer/maker and crafts writer who is completely obsessed with felt! She's the author of two books about felt crafting: *Super-Cute Felt* (CICO Books, 2011) and *Super-Cute Felt Animals* (Cima Books, 2013). Laura shares free tutorials and writes about her crafty adventures on her blog bugsandfishes.blogspot.com and sells her work at lupin.bigcartel.com

KAJSA KINSELLA

Swedish Kajsa Kinsella is the commissioning editor of *Scandinavian Makes* magazine, a published author, and an established designer. Her work carries a distinct Scandinavian style and is created with the utmost intent of staying true to the Nordic traditions, color schemes, and overall northern "feel." Look for her work and follow her progress at www.thenorthernshores.com.

JANE BAILEY KOHLENSTEIN

Jane Bailey Kohlenstein is the creator of Buzzmills, a blog and Etsy shop. She is the mother of two—from whom she finds crafty inspiration every day. It's been twelve years since she was gifted a sewing machine and eight years since she made her first stuffed animal. Since then, she has been learning to sew as she goes. Jane started Buzzmills three years ago as an outlet for her creativity and to regain a sense of self after transitioning from life as a working mom in New York City to a stay-at-home mom in the 'burbs. She finds her head constantly filled with ideas. She can be found on her blog or crafting or sewing something nearly every day. When she's not buried under fabric, she enjoys gardening, hiking, and satisfying her children's creative whims.

ASHLEY LITTLE

Ashley Little is a writer and editor who left her job at Martha Stewart to freelance in the mountains of Asheville, North Carolina. She has her hands in all kinds of crafts, from knitting to crocheting and sewing. Her work has appeared on awesome craft sites such as Whimseybox.com and Craftsy.com, and she's the author of Lark's *Chunky Knits* book (2014). See what Ashley is making at her blog, TheFeistyRedhead.blogspot.com.

SUZIE MILLIONS

Suzie Millions is an artist and compulsive crafter. Her book, *The Complete Book of Retro Crafts*, was published by Lark in 2008. Her studio is profiled in the 2010 book *Where Women Create: Book of Inspiration: In the Studio & Behind the Scenes with Extraordinary Women*. She is a frequent contributor to other Lark books, and her Felty Family Portraits are featured on Martha Stewart's Living blog: livingblog.marthastewart.com/2012/06/how-to-felty-family-portraits.html. See more of her work at suziemillions.com and behance.net/suewille.

CHIARA ALBERETTI MILOTT

Drawing on a background in Fine Arts (BA in Fine Art from Skidmore College, MFA from the School of Visual Arts, NYC), Chiara has always had an eye for beauty and a love of creating and crafting. Working at Martha Stewart Living Omnimedia as a prop stylist inspired and strengthened her desire to create beautiful things. Several years and two little boys later, she still loves creating and making pretty things. Find out more about Chiara at chiarabelle.com, check out what she has been making at etsy.com/shop/chiarabelle, and see all her DIY projects on ohhappyday.com.

DORA MORELAND

Dora Moreland has been exposed to different crafts for as long as she can remember. She grew up in Hungary, surrounded by her mother's creations and a culture that highly prizes folk art and crafts. Even though she has lived most of her life in the United States, she still considers herself Hungarian and is influenced by her heritage

Dora's greatest achievements include being a stay-at-home mom to five children whom she home-schools, volunteering as a Cub Scout leader and still managing to cook dinner on most days. She loves to read, craft, sew, and make jewelry and toys for her children. *Craft Camp* is her second collaboration with Lark Crafts. She is a contributor to *Make Your Mark: Creative Ideas Using Markers, Paint Pens, Bleach Pens & More* (2014). Dora is a co-author at http://bluefishonabike.blogspot.com and has a small Etsy shop (Paul Street Shop) where she sells a few of her creations, including some fun printables for wooden peg people. She also writes a personal blog (plentyofpaprika.blogspot.com) where she shares Hungarian food, crafts, and family life.

JOHN MURPHY

John Murphy is a behavioral counselor for at-risk teenagers and maintains an active

art career. He is the author of *Stupid Sock Creatures, Closet Monsters,* and *Return of the Stupid Sock Creatures* (both by Lark Books), and has co-written several other how-to titles about stuffed toys. John designs toys for The Land of Nod and is a compulsive doodler. Find out more about John and his work at www.stupidcreatures.com.

SARAH OLMSTED

Sarah grew up in Colorado and spent much of her time exploring art, science, and the nearby foothills and mountains. After receiving a bachelor of fine arts degree from the San Francisco Art Institute, she spent some time as a freelance children's furniture designer/ fabricator, which eventually led her to the Field Museum of Natural History. There she worked in exhibit design, developing interactive educational activities for permanent and traveling exhibitions before moving on to co-found imaginechildhood.com in 2008. Sarah is the author of *Imagine Childhood: Exploring the World Through Nature, Imagination and Play—25 Projects that Spark Curiosity and Adventure* (Roost Books, 2012).

AIMEE RAY

Graphic designer and illustrator Aimee Ray is the bestselling author of the *Doodle Stitching* series of hand-embroidery books, in addition to contributing numerous projects and instructions to many Lark titles. She runs the successful Etsy store LittleDear, with almost 10,000 followers, and also maintains her popular blog LittleDearTracks.blogspot.com. She lives in northwestern Arkansas with her husband and children.

JENNIFER RODRIGUEZ

Jennifer Rodriguez is a mother of three, wife, and artist in West Jordan, Utah. On most early mornings and late nights, she can be found creating textile art and mixed-media creations in her studio. Fueled by Diet Coke and her children's laughter, she is inspired daily to make something meaningful. Her artwork has been featured in *Art Quilting Studio*, *Quilting Arts*, and *Stitch*. Her quilting pattern designs are available on the Moda Bakeshop website as well as Riley Blake's Cutting Corners. From fabric to polymer clay, she is inspired by color and texture. To keep up with her latest adventures, read her blogs at AllThingsBelle.blogspot.com

KARIN SCHAEFER

Since 2011, Karin and ten-year-old Freja have been blogging about crafts for kids and grownups at the Swedish blog Pysselbolaget.se/TheCraftySwedes.com. They want kids and grownups to spend more time together creating things. On their blog they show simple and fun crafts that don't require too much knowledge, equipment, or time. They create most of their crafts out of things that they find at home, and they always work together—always. The magic is found in the collaboration between young and old.

When they are not crafting, Freja loves to play soccer and bake, and Karin makes a living as a graphic designer. They live in the beautiful archipelago of Stockholm.

CYNTHIA SHAFFER

Cynthia Shaffer is a mixed-media artist, creative sewer, and photographer whose love of art can be traced back to childhood. At the age of six, she learned to sew, and in no time was designing and sewing clothing for herself and others. After earning a degree in textiles from California State University, Long Beach, Cynthia worked for ten years as the owner of a company that specialized in the design and manufacture of sportswear. Numerous books and magazines have featured Cynthia's art and photography work: she is the author of *Stash Happy Patchwork* (Lark, 2011), *Stash Happy Appliqué* (Lark, 2012), co-author of *Serge It* (Lark 2014), and *Coastal Crafts* (Lark, 2015). In her spare time, Cynthia knits, crochets, paints, and dabbles in all sorts of crafts. If she's not crafting, Cynthia can been found at the gym lifting weights, kick-boxing, or in the back bay of Newport Beach with her paddling friends. Cynthia lives with her husband Scott, sons Corry and Cameron, and beloved dogs Harper and Berklee in Southern California. For more information, visit Cynthia online at cynthiashaffer.typepad.com or www.cynthiashaffer.com.

MARY SINNER

Mary Sinner is a recent MFA graduate of the University of Utah with an emphasis in painting. She has worked as a personal stylist and as a designer for a home-makeover television show.

NORA VRBA

Nora Vrba is an art director and mom and lives with her husband and two daughters in an apartment in Amsterdam. They have a rooftop garden and a cat named Fritz. At the end of November 2011, just when she had decided to quit her job and begin work as a freelance art director, she was diagnosed with breast cancer. After intense treatment, the future looks very promising. The moment Nora started to regain her energy, she needed to do something productive, and she started a little shop called La Fête. Whenever she finds time and inspiration, she designs her own items and makes them herself in small editions or to order. Nora loves to collect and share—that's where the blog about her life and the things she makes and does comes in. See www.la-fete.nl, because every day is worth celebrating

ANNE B. WEIL
Anne B. Weil, the voice and creative mind behind Flax & Twine (www.flaxandtwine.com), is a maker and lover of beautiful things. On her blog, she provides DIYs, patterns, projects, and inspiration to endlessly delight people in their quest for a happy handmade life. Anne creates charming and simple designs in craft, knitting, arm-knitting, finger-knitting, and crocheting. She revels in the peace and

happiness of making things, but as a busy mother of three, she also understands the challenges of finding time. She was a member of Martha Stewart's select team of bloggers for 2014, "12 Months of Martha." Her knitting designs and craftwork can be found in delightful places all across the Web, including Design Sponge, Martha Stewart, Poppytalk, Creature Comforts, Apartment Therapy, Pottery Barn, Huffington Post, Petite Purls, Knit and Crochet Now! and more.

SUSANA ZARCO
Susana Zarco is an industrial designer and teacher at design schools in Barcelona. Interested in crafts, she created the Lots of Loops website (2006) and makes crocheted art pieces, patterns and kits, and craft products for kids. These projects led to the creation of the Barribastall studio/workshop of creative activities (2011) www.lotsofloops.com and www.barribastall.com

KIDS' MASKS
Enlarge by 50%

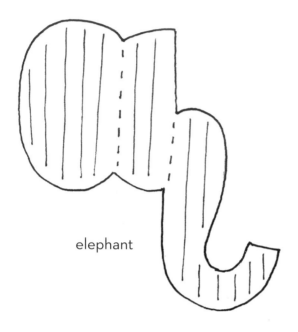

elephant

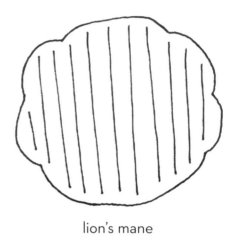

lion's mane

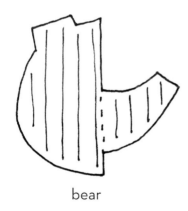

bear

lion's face

MAGNETIC ROBOTS

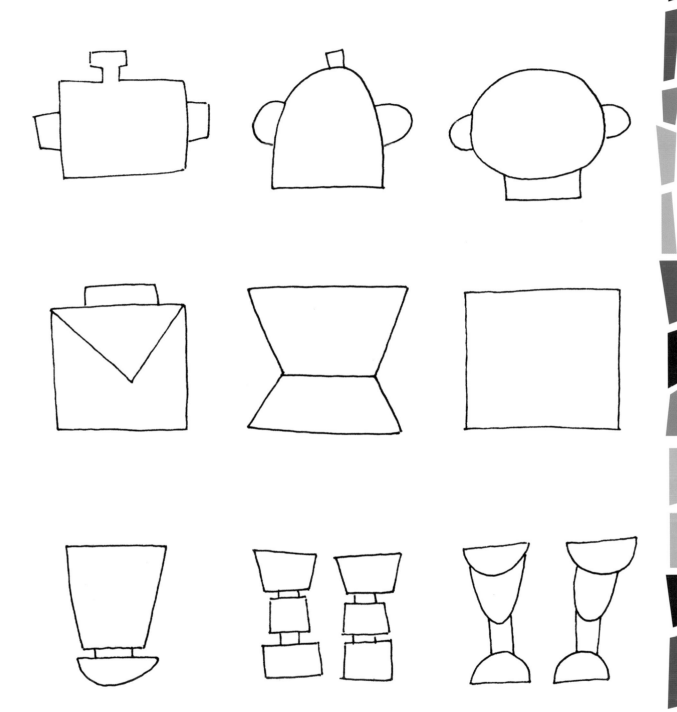

DOG BOWL AND DAD'S MUG

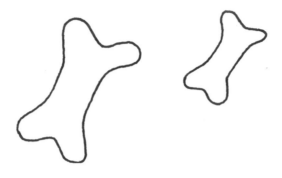

Dog Bowl

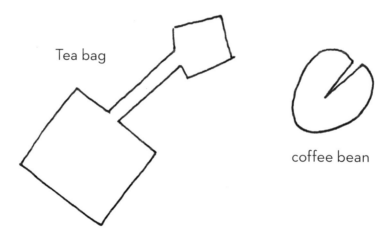

Tea bag

coffee bean

Dad's Mug

APPLIQUÉD FLEECE SCARF

Enlarge by 10%

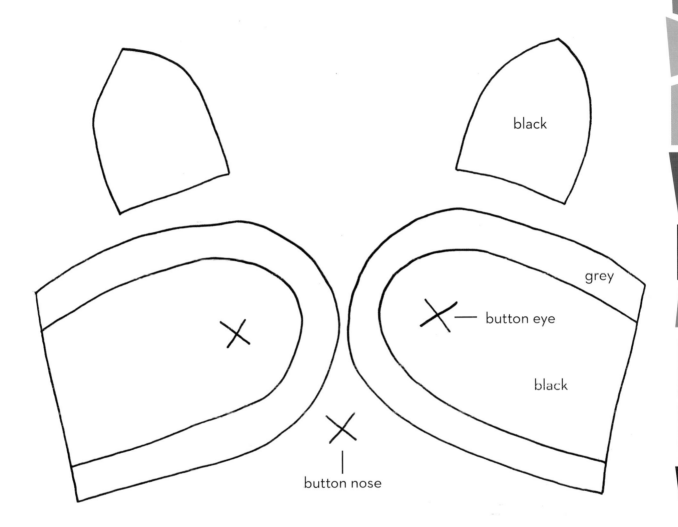

black

grey

— button eye

black

button nose

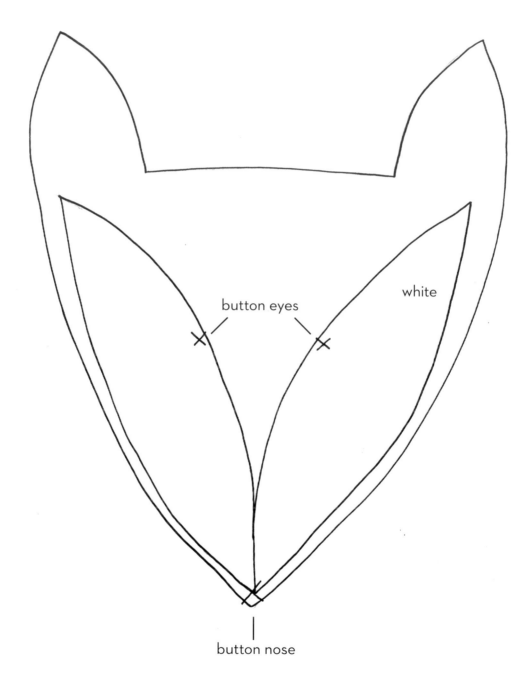

button eyes

white

button nose

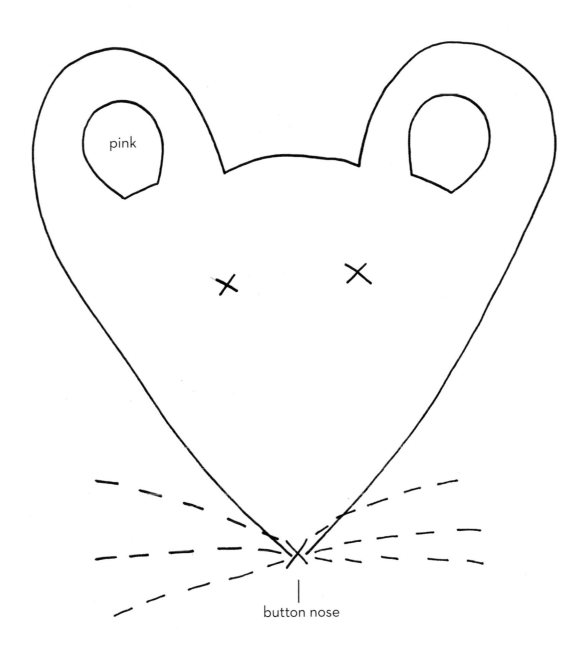

pink

button nose

BIRD TOSS ORNITHOLOGY GAME
Enlarge by 20%

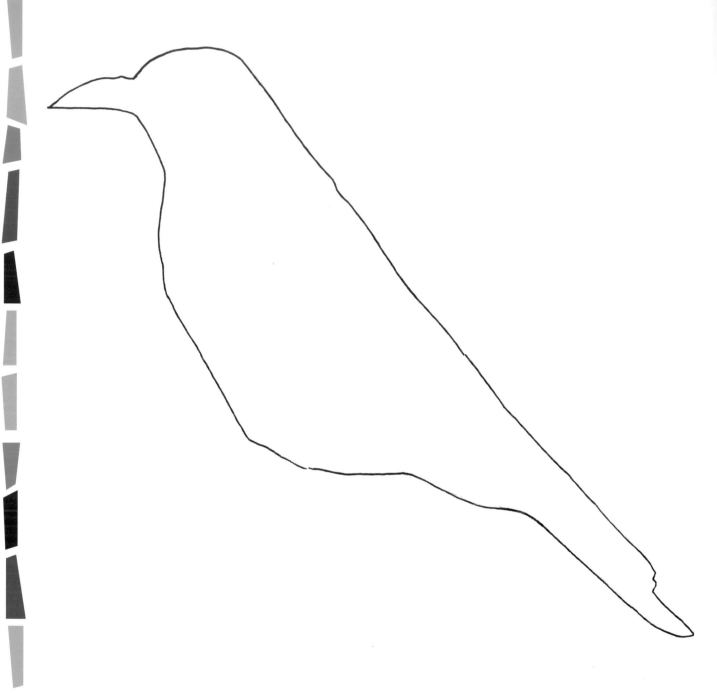

Crow

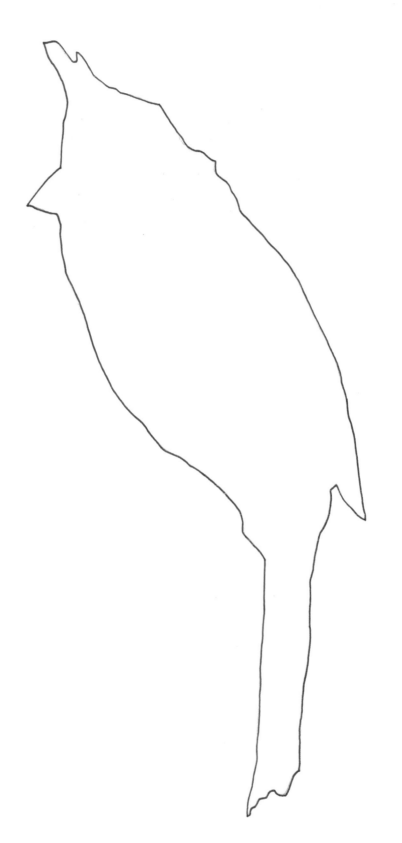

Cardinal

Enlarge by 20%

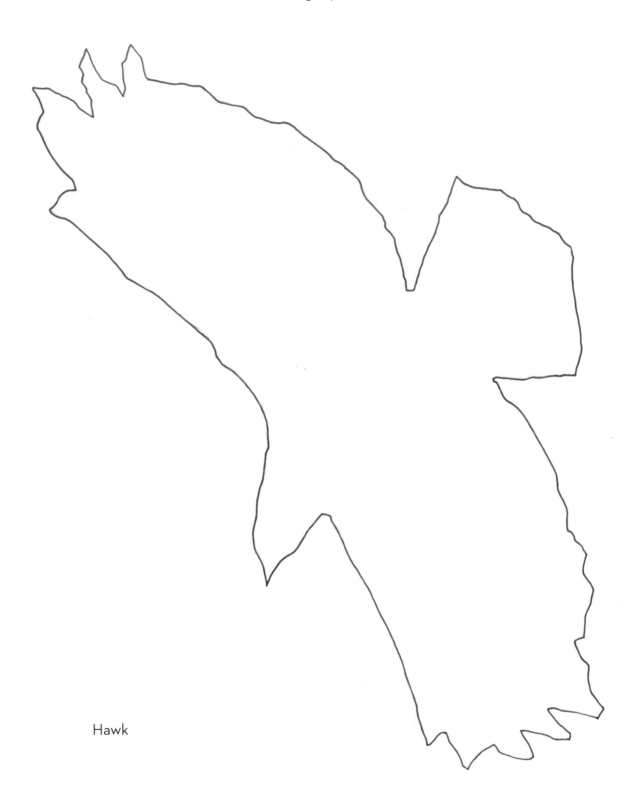

Hawk

Enlarge by 20%

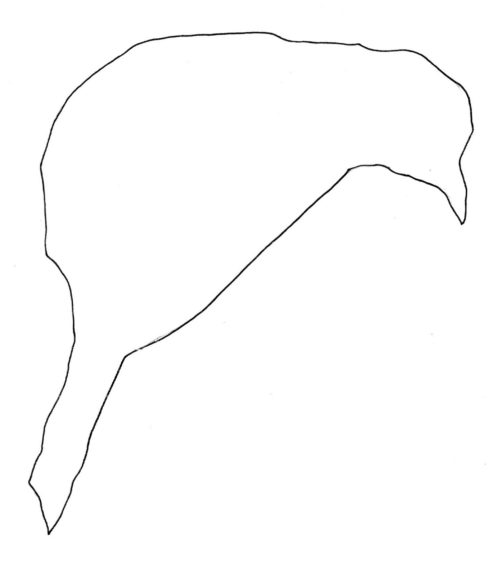

Robin

Enlarge by 20%

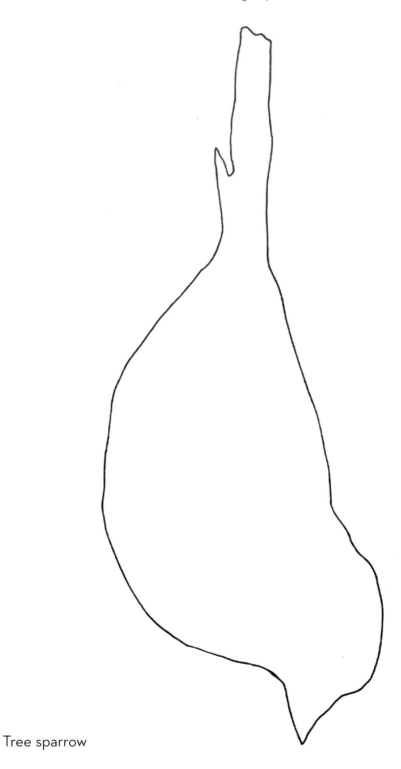

Tree sparrow

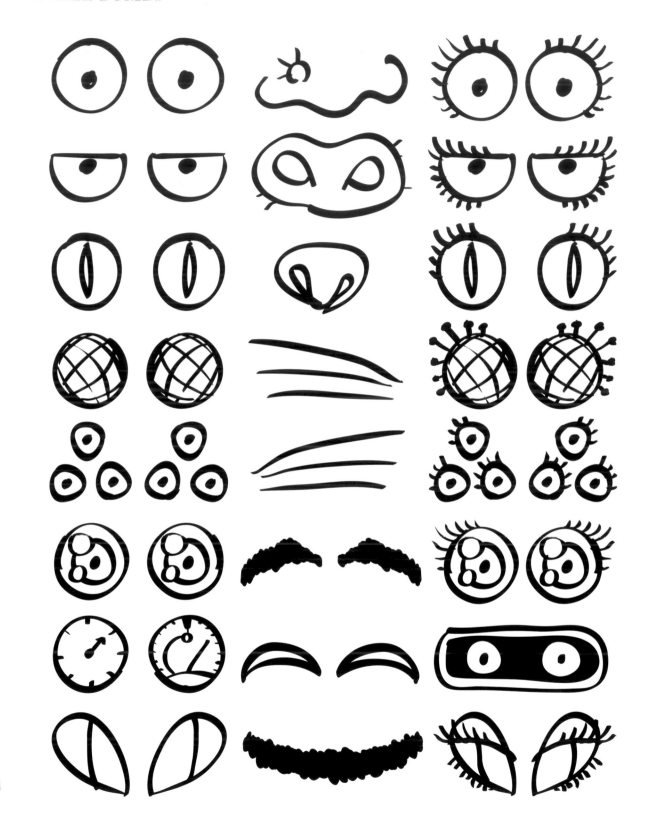

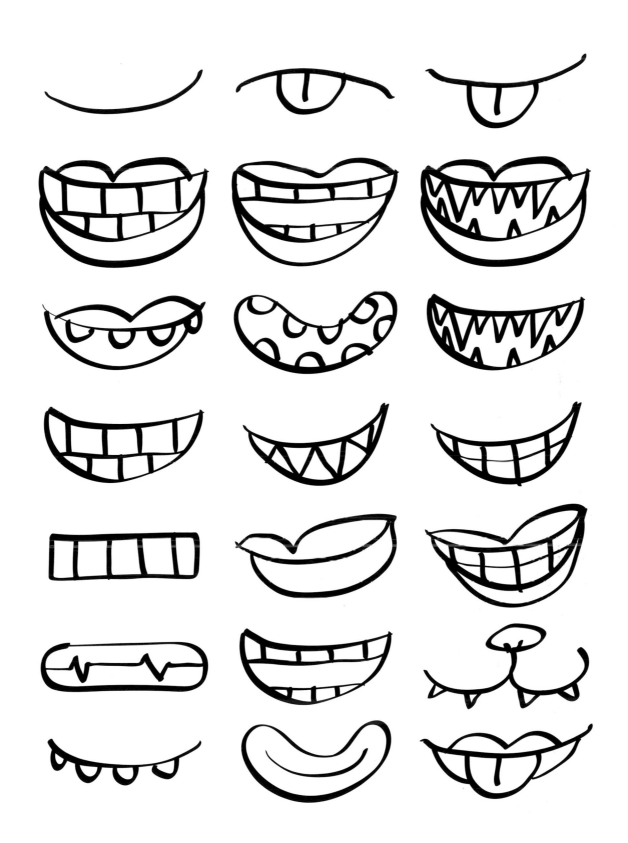

AN OWLY FRIEND

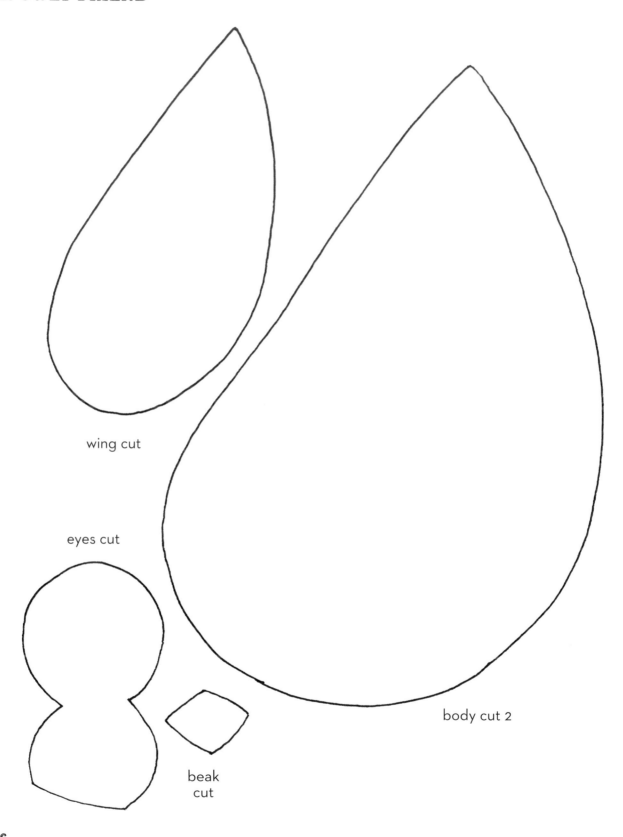

wing cut

eyes cut

beak
cut

body cut 2

136

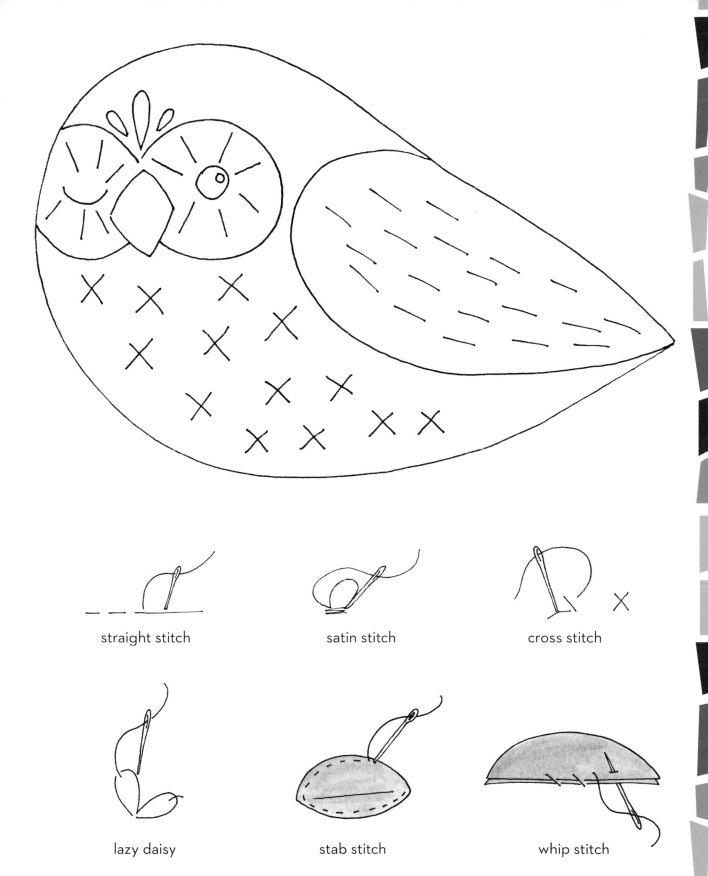

straight stitch

satin stitch

cross stitch

lazy daisy

stab stitch

whip stitch

CRAYON STAINED GLASS

Enlarge by 30%

WATERMELON CROSS STITCH

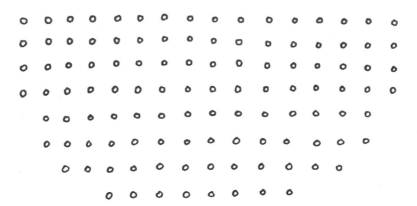

BITTY BEAVER

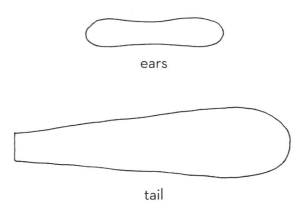

ears

tail

INDEX

Note: Page numbers in *italics* indicate projects and templates (in parentheses). Page numbers in **bold** indicate contributor information. Project titles with asterisks (*) require adult supervision.